STABBED IN THE FRONT

Post-war General Elections
through political cartoons

Alan Mumford

With a foreword by
Rt Hon Lord Kenneth Baker

Cartoons

Centre for the Study of Cartoons and Caricature
University of Kent at Canterbury

Cover illustration:

Ralph Steadman's cartoon was originally published in the *New Statesman* of 11
April 1997, in the middle of the General Election campaign. A phalanx of naked
pollsters and pundits - led by a grotesque graph-headed creature - interrogates
two ordinary voters, described in the accompanying article as "fart fodder...for
the enormous volume of odoriferous pooting and puffing that's going to continue
for the next month."

Designed, printed and bound in the UK by E.C.Parker Ltd, Canterbury Kent
on environmentally friendly paper from sustainable resources.

UNIVERSITY OF KENT
AT CANTERBURY ■■■■

The Centre for the Study of Cartoons and Caricature is pleased to be publishing Alan Mumford's *Stabbed in the Front* as an important addition to the study of British Electioneering since 1945, and a valuable contribution to the General Election campaign of 2001.

The Centre was established at the University of Kent at Canterbury in 1973, to encourage the preservation and study of this neglected branch of creative art. Its work involves the archiving and cataloguing of major collections of cartoons from newspapers and magazines, the organising of exhibitions, the provision of images for research and publication, and the production of books such as *Stabbed in the Front*.

The Centre is not only an archive, but also a picture library and a research centre. It specialises in images of social and political comment, and currently holds more than 80,000 original cartoons and caricatures, plus a collection of 70,000 newspaper cuttings of social and political cartoons, and a photographic archive of almost 60,000 images. The Centre's computer database of 40,000 cartoons is freely available on the web at http://library.ukc.ac.uk/cartoons/.

The Centre encourages the study of cartoons and caricature across the whole of UK Higher Education. It is currently leading the *CartoonHub* project, funded by the Higher Education Funding Councils, to catalogue cartoons from the University of Kent, the National Library of Wales, the London School of Economics, and the John Rylands University Library of Manchester. The Centre is also working on a project funded by the Arts and Humanities Research Board, to add 65,000 catalogued images to its online database by the year 2004.

The Centre for the Study of Cartoons and Caricature relies on loans and donations of work from newspapers and magazines, from cartoonists and their families, and from collectors. We are grateful to all those who have supported us in the past, and hope that they will find their enthusiasm for British cartooning reflected in the pages of *Stabbed in the Front*.

Dr Nicholas Hiley
Head of the Centre for the Study of Cartoons and Caricature
University of Kent at Canterbury
Canterbury CT2 7NU
tel/fax 01227 823127
email N.P.Hiley@ukc.ac.uk

BY JOVE!
I MUST LET
EVERYBODY
KNOW ABOUT THIS!

STRUBE

The author

Alan Mumford is an expert on how managers learn, and he has written a number of books on this subject. This is his first book on political cartoons, a field in which he has an extensive collection of books and original cartoons.

He was first involved in politics at the University of Cambridge, where, at the time of the Suez campaign, he was hit by a tomato during a rowdy Union Society debate. He sees cartoons as a physically more gentle but psychologically more damaging form of attack.

Contents

Acknowledgements

The opportunity of writing this book was provided by the attention given to me by the medical staff at the Walsgrave Hospital, Coventry. My friend Peter Honey then suggested that I turn a fantasy into a writing project, and my wife Denise encouraged me in carrying the work through to publication.

The Rt Hon Lord Kenneth Baker of Dorking C.H. encouraged me in my original idea, and then took on the task of persuading politicians to contribute to the book. Without his enthusiasm and commitment *Stabbed in the Front* would not exist in its final form.

My thanks also go to Dr Nicholas Hiley and Jane Newton at the Centre for the Study of Cartoons and Caricature, University of Kent at Canterbury. They developed their enthusiasm for the book into an agreement to act as publisher, and the majority of the images in this book have been taken from the Centre's impressive collection of cartoons. The Centre's involvement with *Stabbed in the Front* has been far greater than that of a normal publisher, and I am grateful for their expertise and generous support.

I would also like to thank all those cartoonists, their families, and other copyright owners, who have generously given permission for these cartoons to appear. Particular thanks are due to Ralph Steadman, for providing such a wonderful cover.

I am greatly indebted to the following who have contributed recollections of General Elections in which they were involved:

Rt Hon Lord Kenneth Baker
Rt Hon Lord James Callaghan
Rt Hon Baroness Barbara Castle
Rt Hon Tony Blair MP
Rt Hon Lord Denis Healey
Rt Hon Sir Edward Heath MP
Rt Hon Lord Roy Jenkins
Rt Hon Lord Longford
Rt Hon John Major MP
Rt Hon Lord James Prior
Lord Tom Sawyer
Rt Hon Lord David Steel
Rt Hon Lord Norman Tebbit
Rt Hon Baroness Margaret Thatcher

A number of political cartoonists also contributed comments either in writing or through interview, and my thanks for this valuable help go to Steve Bell, Stanley Franklin, Nick Garland, Les Gibbard, John Jensen, Martin Rowson, and Ralph Steadman.

Foreword
by Lord Baker of Dorking

One can certainly chart the history of the General Elections of last fifty years through political cartoons: they depict the passing moment. Some of those moments are memorable and will live on in history, some soon fade. But what they all do is to capture the mood of the moment and the standing of individual politicians.

Elections start with manifestos - that is the written word - and most parties regret having printed them as the promises become albatrosses. No politician would dare to admit in the frankness of Jonathan Swift that "promises are like piecrusts, made to be broken". But elections are more than words, pictures count as well. The daily cartoons throughout an election leave more vivid impressions in the elector's mind than columns of newsprint.

Kenneth Baker by KAL

An election without cartoons would be a dull and naked affair. These cartoons go back to 1945 and help to bring those faraway elections back to life. The period after the Second World War was a very rich one for political cartooning. David Low, who had campaigned in his cartoons against the Fascists and the appeasers in the 1930s, was still drawing. Although he was well to the Left of centre - the phrase used in those days was Socialist - he had a great respect for Churchill because of his stance in the 1930s and for his heroic leadership which had defeated Fascism.

There was also "Vicky", a refugee from Hungary, with strong left-wing sympathies who took on from where David Low left off. One of his most famous creations was of Harold Macmillan as "Supermac" - a superman with tights and cloak, swooping over Gaitskell. It was meant to be ironic, but Vicky had in fact created an attractive image of Macmillan which helped him to win the 1959 Election. The cartoonist on the right was Cummings who drew for the *Express* and the *Standard*, and more latterly the *Daily Mail*: he created a whole political landscape of his own, as did "Jak" in the *Evening Standard*.

In the 1960s, Gerald Scarfe and Ralph Steadman introduced a degree of raw, vulgar humour with their slashing attacks upon Wilson and Heath - bare bottoms, vomiting and defecation were back.

Then a new generation of cartoonists appeared. Most notably Martin Rowson and Steve Bell in the *Guardian*. They are Socialist to the core - indeed Rowson has a

statue of Lenin in his sitting room. Steve Bell created an image of John Major - which I think will endure - of him wearing naff, white, aertex y-fronts over his trousers. These underpants went on to become parachutes, bags, gags, door mats, hats, and buckets. These two cartoonists detest Tony Blair even more than John Major, and they make the most of Blair's big grin and teeth.

Throughout all that period Nick Garland was at the *Telegraph* - his cartoons were witty and elegant. More latterly we have Peter Brookes at the *Times* who has transformed through his "Nature Notes" politicians of all political parties into plants, animals and insects. And there is also Charles Griffin, Richard Willson, John Jensen and Stan McMurtry.

Politicians have a love/hate relationship with cartoonists. They love to appear in cartoons and indeed for a rising politician it is a sign he has arrived. On the other hand, they wince when the darts hit home. Churchill did not like the cartoons which depicted him in during his second premiership as an old man, only fleetingly in charge of events. Anthony Eden used to ring up his Chief Whip, Ted Heath, every day to complain about the press coverage and the cartoons. Margaret Thatcher could not care less. She was depicted in many vicious and unkind ways, but she did not even bother to look at them. Few of her Prime Ministerial colleagues have had that aloof disdain - more's the pity for them.

Introduction

Origins.

The title of this book is partly a political quotation, and partly an homage to "Vicky" - Victor Weisz - the first cartoonist to really attract my attention as I became interested in politics. At the Labour Party Conference of 1947, Ernest Bevin, the Foreign Secretary, claimed that he had been "stabbed in the back" by left-wing opponents of his foreign policy, and in 1952 Vicky borrowed Bevin's words for a collection of his post-war cartoons entitled *Stabs in the Back*. I have however changed the positioning of the "stab", because although they may be seen as unfair, political cartoons are an obvious assault from the front, not a covert attack from the rear.

This book is a history of British General Elections since 1945, seen through the eyes of political cartoonists. A separate chapter is devoted to each post-war General Election, with a range of political cartoons from different sources, and background information on the context of the Election and the major issues of the campaign. As it seemed unlikely that most readers would know all the politicians in the cartoons, I have provided a short biographical profile of the major figures depicted. I have also made a personal choice of the "Cartoonist of the Election" in these cases with other details from Mark Bryant's admirable *Dictionary of Twentieth-Century British Cartoonists and Caricaturists* (London, Ashgate, 2000).

Criteria for Selection.

It was not easy to decide which political cartoons should be included in this book. There were thousands from which to choose, published throughout the daily and Sunday newspapers and the major weeklies and monthlies over the months of Electioneering. It is not always easy to determine when a General Election starts, for politicians often seem to begin fighting the next Election as soon as the last one is over. However, for this study I have taken as my starting point the day the Prime Minister announced the date of the General Election, and I have confined myself to cartoons published between then and the declaration of the result.

In selecting the individual cartoons a number of different criteria were used. I have deliberately chosen full-sized cartoons - not pocket or strip cartoons - that had national circulation throughout the United Kingdom. One exception is the inclusion of cartoons from the London *Evening Standard*, on the grounds that although not a national newspaper it had an impact on a significant proportion of the population, and was read by many politicians based in London. Despite their small circulations, I have also included the *Daily Worker* and the *Morning Star*, as few other journals have produced savage cartoons more widely critical of established politics.

In selecting the cartoons I have made no attempt to secure balance between those attacking or supporting the different political parties, as - fortunately or unfortunately depending on one's political loyalties - this criterion would have been at odds with the others. In discussing the subject of this book, Dave Brown, cartoonist for the *Independent*, supported the image of the cartoonist as participant in the Election campaign, assuring me that "I have no intention either to promote or refrain from criticising one party or another, however neither do I see my role as being an impartial reporter. To have any power the political cartoon must surely represent the cartoonist's personal beliefs, rather than simply being an uncommitted topical gag."

I have deliberately chosen cartoons that still have the power to make me wince, or make me laugh, but humour was also not one of the major criteria. The political cartoon is differentiated from the social cartoon in that whilst the latter is more often than not intended to raise a smile - if not a laugh - the political cartoon often has no such intention. David Low, who drew for Beaverbrook's *Evening Standard*, argued in favour of ridicule and mockery as the prime emphasis in cartoons, but other political cartoonists have been dismissive of the idea that anybody should laugh at their work.

I have also chosen cartoons that dealt with situations, events, or issues of significance during the Election campaign, rather than caricatures of single individuals. The artistic quality of the drawing was not one of my criteria, as I do not have the knowledge or sensitivity to make a selection of that sort. It is likely that instead of artistic merit I have more often chosen cartoons for their simplicity both of drawing and intent - cartoons either crammed too full of detail or of ideas did not seem to make a strong case for inclusion.

My policy of selection is perhaps best summed up by Professor Colin Seymour-Ure, who has contributed so much to our understanding of political cartoons. As he explains, "cartoons can be seen as having three purposes in a General Election": "They monitor the progress of the campaign, reflecting the activities of participants. Secondly, they interpret the campaign, setting it in context and evaluating it. Thirdly, cartoonists can offer approval or disapproval; in which case they become participants themselves, most obviously on the side of a particular party" (*Political Communications*, 1986, p.170). Cartoons do not, of course, tell the whole story - for example, the nationalist campaigns in

Wales, Scotland and Northern Ireland are not represented in this collection, for even in 1997 few cartoons were available on this subject.

Newspapers and Magazines.

The selection of cartoons was also determined by the number of newspapers that employed political cartoonists during each General Election. In 1945, despite newsprint rationing and the relatively small size of newspapers, the popular newspapers all employed political cartoonists. Yet this was not an enduring rule, and some newspapers had cartoonists for some General Elections but not others. The *Daily Mirror* for example had no political cartoonist in 1950 or 1951, whilst the *News of the World*, with the largest circulation of any Sunday newspaper, seemed unconcerned whether it did or did not employ a political cartoonist during a General Election. Perhaps more than any other newspaper this may have been due to its diligent concentration on other aspects of British life.

Even the broadsheets did not employ a political cartoonist for every post-war General Election. The 1955 Election was the first in which the *Guardian* employed a staff cartoonist - it had recruited David Low in 1953 - and the *Observer* was even later in the field, employing its first staff cartoonist only in the 1959 Election. *The Times* and the *Sunday Times* were even further behind, as they first employed staff cartoonists for the 1970 Election - when *The Times* may have surprised its readers by choosing Ralph Steadman. There were equal anomalies among the weekly magazines. *Punch* of course had a century-long tradition of political cartooning, whilst *Tribune* had its own political cartoonist - though not of first rank - by 1945. However, the *New Statesman* did not carry cartoons until the 1955 General Election, when it employed Vicky, and the *Spectator* waited until 1959, when it employed "Trog" - Wally Fawkes.

The size of cartoons and their positioning in the paper also varied between different newspapers and different periods. Most often they appeared either on the same page as the Editorial or on the opposite page, although the London *Evening Standard* has always carried its political cartoon on the "Diary" page. However, during General Election campaigns political cartoons have sometimes appeared on the front page - or even, in the *Guardian*, on the back page - as a direct intervention into the news. The way each cartoonist addresses his audience has also varied between newspapers, and over time. A detailed study of differences in style and content between tabloid and broadsheet cartoons would be illuminating, but no research on this is available.

There were also major differences in the size and circulation of newspapers and magazines during the post-war period, and political cartoons must be seen against the general background of the British news media, which have changed significantly over time.

The significance of radio Election broadcasts may strike many modern readers as strange, as most of us now rely on television broadcasts - if indeed we watch or listen to anything at all. Yet in the General Election of 1945 many political cartoonists still picked up their ideas from radio broadcasting and from the newspaper reactions to it. Party Political Broadcasts did not reach television until the General Election of 1951, and then only one in ten of the population was able to receive them. Yet since then television has had a major impact not only on the conduct of General Elections, but also on the way in which cartoonists have portrayed them.

The Longevity of Political Cartoonists.

The cartoonists themselves have remained remarkably stable against this changing background. It is possible to argue that even the more extreme cartoonists match the comment made by the Glaswegian Marxist in Trevor Griffiths' 1974 play *The Party*, who criticises the commitment of middle-class Socialists by telling them "You'll bite the hand that feeds you - but you'll not bite it off." In a discussion of British political cartooning, Martin Rowson admitted to me that in the past he has not been even-handed in his criticism, and has been anti-Tory - although his disappointment with the Labour Government has now begun to show. However, his belief is that politicians and cartoonists need each other, and that their needs tend to cancel each other out. Politicians need the attention, but cartoonists need the subjects, and any criticism made by the cartoonist tends to be balanced by the attention the politician gets. Rowson may be extremely rude about politicians he likes personally, but unlike some cartoonists he does not dislike them as a class - he says that, as in Francis Ford Coppola's 1972 film *The Godfather*, "It's just business".

This tacit understanding has allowed British political cartoonists a long and productive working life - right from the days of John Tenniel and later Bernard Partridge on *Punch*. David Low and Sidney Strube both began drawing political cartoons before the First World War, and were still doing so after the Second World War. Michael Cummings drew first for *Tribune* in 1948, then for the *Daily Express* and *Sunday Express,* and the *Times Weekend*, right up to the 1997 General Election.

Gerald Scarfe's first General Election cartoons appeared in the *Daily Sketch* in 1959 - though in a rather different style from his later work - and he is still drawing. Trog - one of many political cartoonists who came to Britain from abroad - started publishing cartoons in 1959 and is also still drawing.

Some of this longevity may have been due to the political flexibility of cartoonists - or to their willingness to change employers in line with their changing political beliefs. Cummings moved from the very left-wing *Tribune* newspaper to Beaverbrook's *Express* group, after which it became difficult to believe that he could ever have been the cartoonist on a left-wing journal. In the 1970s Nicholas Garland drew for the left-wing *New Statesman*, but he now draws for both the conventionally right-wing *Daily Telegraph* and the less conventionally right-wing *Spectator*. But a move between newspapers may not be attributable to straightforward political inclination. As Dr Tim Benson's research has shown, Low's transfer from the *Evening Standard* to the *Daily Herald* in 1950 was not caused by political disagreement - though perhaps his later move from the *Herald* to the *Guardian* did relate to a substantial level of discomfort.

However, it would be wrong to suggest that cartoonists always reflect the opinions of the papers for which they work. In the 1940s Vicky had so many of his cartoons rejected by his employer, the *News Chronicle*, that he published them in book form under the title *The Editor Regrets*. Equally, the fact that Scarfe was employed on the *Mail* and the *Sunday Times* in the 1960s, and that Steadman was the first major political cartoonist on *The Times* in the 1970s, are most remarkable for the shock which their cartoons must have caused to many regular readers. Yet many papers seem to have been able to absorb these creative tensions. When asked about his experiences on the *Sunday Telegraph* in the 1960s and 1970s, John Jensen told me that he had never had a cartoon rejected, although at Election time there was always a certain amount of pressure on him not to be too anti-Tory.

To some extent these tensions were affected by whether the cartoonist submitted just one cartoon or rough drawing to the editor, or submitted several. This certainly seems to have helped on the *Daily Express* in the 1980s, where the editor, Derek Jameson, described his cartoonist Cummings as "slightly to the right of Attila the Hun": "He reserves most of his venom for Labour leaders. Every day he submits five or six rough outlines and I select the one which seems least cruel." (*Last of the Hot Metal Men* 1990, p.55) However, submitting roughs is not always the best way of defusing tensions between an editor and a cartoonist. Martin Rowson recalled of the 1980s that "when I worked briefly as editorial cartoonist on *Today*, every rough for a cartoon I presented to him was rejected by David Montgomery as a matter of course, to keep me in my place with the rest of the hacks." (*British Journalism Review*, 2001, p.32) The truth seems to be that whilst few

cartoonists suffer rejection for failing to fit in with a newspaper's political line, they mostly migrate to papers with which they have a reasonable degree of political sympathy.

References, Symbols and Metaphors.

Other changes and continuities can be seen in the metaphors and symbols used by British political cartoonists during General Elections. At one time it was possible to draw these references from a narrow cultural range, and the fact that Gerald Barry, editor of the *News Chronicle*, instructed Vicky to steep himself in Dickens and Shakespeare in order to become a successful British cartoonist is well-known. Vicky came from Hungary, and - unlike the other Fleet Street expatriates from New Zealand, Australia and Canada - would have had no significant exposure to the canon of British literature. Yet the use of literary references is declining, as is shown in the relatively small number that appear in this book - only Garland is still regularly using such references in his work.

The absence of literary references in the later Election campaigns may be more of a comment on newspaper readers than on newspaper cartoonists. It could have been as a compliment to his readership that Low drew a cartoon involving the Greek philosopher Diogenes during the 1945 Election campaign, but he must have expected that they would understand the reference. His 1959 General Election cartoon based on Auguste Rodin's sculpture "The Thinker" also assumed that readers of the *Manchester Guardian* were familiar with such high cultural references, as did Papas' *Guardian* cartoon from the 1964 General Election, which used a Latin tag as its title. No such assumptions are made nowadays, and although metaphor continues to be used by political cartoonists in General Elections, it is most often drawn from a sporting rather than a literary context - especially with reference to starting the political race.

The lack of common symbols is also noticeable. It is interesting that there are no British equivalents of the Democratic Donkey and the Republican Elephant used by American cartoonists to represent the main political parties. Low did like to represent the TUC as a carthorse, but it is noticeably absent from his General Election cartoons. The Conservative and Labour Parties may have a continuous history, but political cartoonists tend to portray them only through their most recent leaders and supporters. There are equally few representations of the common man, despite his significance to all General Election campaigns. Before the Second World War, Sidney Strube had used his "Little Man" to make comments within a cartoon, and Low's "Colonel Blimp" had been an equally famous running character commenting on political events. Low

and Vicky even appeared as critical commentators in their own cartoons, but today only Franklin's character "Raspberry" remains to offer a sideways glance at political events.

Cartoonists may represent British political parties through individuals, but those individuals are in turn usually identified through some specific characteristic, or item of dress. Churchill's liking for a variety of different hats was often the subject of political cartoons, and if that characteristic is not represented in this book, his love of cigars certainly is. No cartoonist has gone so far as to identify Churchill solely through his cigar, with no representation of the man himself, but in the eyes of cartoonists the two were inseparable. It was certainly to his detriment that Churchill's rival Attlee provided no such easily-identifiable mark for political cartoonists.

The connection with smoking was continued with Harold Wilson. In private life Wilson might actually have preferred to smoke cigars rather than a pipe - and to drink brandy rather than beer - but in cartoons his pipe was ever present. Wilson also became associated with a particular kind of coat - a Gannex mackintosh - which became such a useful identifier for cartoonists that it frequently appeared in circumstances where a coat would not have been needed. Michael Foot in turn became associated with another sort of coat, after being savagely attacked for wearing an inappropriate garment - inaccurately described as a donkey jacket - at an Armistice Day ceremony. With equal regularity Foot's use of a stick, and the accompaniment of his dog, were employed in portraying him as a feeble leader.

Margaret Thatcher would have appeared a strong person in any context, although in the early days of her public career cartoonists generally identified her by her hats. These were no longer a feature of her public image by the time of the 1979 General Election, when political cartoonists chose to focus either on the famous description of her as "an Iron Lady", or on the handbag with which she was supposed to hit people. The contrast between Thatcher and her successor John Major was as vivid in cartoons as it was in real life, and Steve Bell's representation of Major through

his underpants was a piece of lese-majesty unthinkable for Thatcher. This portrayal carried echoes of one of the most famous political cartoon images - Vicky's ironic depiction of Harold Macmillan as "Supermac". Major's rival and successor, Tony Blair, was originally portrayed as the Disney fawn "Bambi", but was later identified entirely by his ever-present smile illuminated by gleaming teeth - and sometimes by his protruding ears.

The Impact of Cartoons on General Elections.

The impact of such representations is difficult to gauge, but Tom Sawyer, General Secretary of the Labour Party during the 1997 General Election campaign, has offered his thoughts on political cartooning for this book. During that campaign Sawyer remained in the Labour campaign office in London, and had a different perspective on cartoons from Labour politicians travelling around the country. "Cartoons are essentially about mood and nuance", he explains, "sometimes they capture it perfectly, and when they do people in politics feel angry or elated depending on how you view the cartoon":

> "The Labour Party had failed to win an election in eighteen years and, with a new leader and the Tories in disarray, there seemed a strong chance that this bad run might end. The stakes were so high, however, that Labour fought like the underdog. This is the background against which all political news including cartoons must be viewed.
>
> The story of Major's demise and the arrival of New Labour New Blair was perhaps the big change about to take place in British politics and the cartoonists got this for themselves. News management is one key skill at the Party's command. In theory during an election campaign the parties, through their daily press conferences, attempt to make the news. One of Labour's strong attack lines was Tory sleaze. So you would expect news stories and cartoons to pick up on this theme and so they did.
>
> My opinion is that campaign managers and their top team are not influenced by cartoons. These people plough their own aims and are single minded about that agenda. I would say, however, that for the Labour Party, the *Guardian* is important in that it is read by most party members and that it would be the morning read of most staff in the

War Room. Consequently, a big hit on the Tories - such as Steve Bell's cartoon on sleaze of 9 April 1997 - would attract comments and put party workers in a confident mood."

This sort of anecdotal evidence is valuable, for although there has been research into the general impact of the press on General Elections, nothing has been published in Britain on the particular impact of political cartoons. Evidence of that impact might be expected from a number of sources, including the memoirs of politicians, the autobiographies of newspaper editors, the histories of individual newspapers, and academic studies of particular General Elections. Yet these sources contain remarkably few references to political cartoons and cartoonists. The memoirs of post-war politicians may include cartoons as illustrations, but there is little about them in the text. Journalists are equally silent, and neither Harold Evans nor Andrew Neil mention Scarfe in their published recollections of editing the *Sunday Times*. The historians follow the same pattern. Edward Hyam's history of the *New Statesman* makes no mention of Vicky, whilst John Grigg's volume of *The History of the Times*, covering 1966 to 1981, has references to the pocket cartoons of Calman and Marc, but nothing on the political cartoons of Steadman, Richard Cole, or Richard Willson.

This lack of evidence is often concealed beneath assertion. Newspapers of course like to think that they have a tremendous impact on General Elections, and are often supported in this by politicians upset by particular aspects of their political coverage. On polling day in the 1992 General Election, the *Sun* published a cartoon-like photomontage on its front page, showing Neil Kinnock's head inside a light bulb beneath the headline "If Kinnock Wins Today Will the Last Person in Britain Please Turn Out the Lights". After the somewhat unexpected Tory victory, the paper claimed in a headline "It's the Sun wot won it". Yet even the *Sun's* political editor, Trevor Kavanagh, is cautious about this, and recently admitted that "There are two totally contradictory academic reports on this. One concluded that we could perhaps sway 2% of the voters in a certain direction, while the other said we have no effect at all. I think you should see instead us as pushing at an open door. If the country's mood is going one way, and so are we, then I guess we might have an effect on some of our readers, confirming their prejudices at the time." (*Guardian*, 2 October 2000, p.2)

There is also a question of how far cartoonists themselves believe they have an impact, particularly during General Elections. Here an element of doubt creeps in. "Drawing politicians over and over again is a tedious business", wrote Gerald Scarfe in his 1986 collection *Scarfe by Scarfe*: "Incidentally, people ask me, do I think my drawings change anything? Answer: 'Not a jot.' So, why do I bother? I don't know. I feel I must cry out - perhaps it can raise the public conscience, prick the public nerve." (*Scarfe by Scarfe*, 1986, n.p.) Ralph

Steadman also dislikes drawing cartoons of politicians, for in his view they feel flattered by them - although it is difficult to imagine politicians seeking to buy the originals of most Steadman cartoons. In 1988 he issued a manifesto to encourage other cartoonists to follow his example, explaining later that "I urged all cartoonists worldwide to stop drawing politicians. I considered that if all cartoonists did that, even for one year, politicians as we know them would change: if we denied them the benefit of our attention, insight and wit, they would suffer withdrawal symptoms of such withering magnitude that the effect on their egos could only be guessed at. Not even a tyrant can survive the whiplash of indifference." (*Observer Magazine*, 27 December 1992, p.7)

In the absence of significant research - or indeed of autobiographical or other comment - it seems sensible to fall back on commonsense. A General Election campaign and the associated media interest - including political cartoons - may play a role in sharpening the identification of voters with a particular political party, or against an individual or a party. But the outcome of a General Election is determined over a substantial period of time, not simply during the few weeks of the campaign itself. It would be wrong to expect political cartoons to have a significant effect on voting behaviour, although they may help to focus attention and encapsulate issues during a General Election. As John Sergeant, the BBC's Chief Political Correspondent, acknowledged at the Cartoon Art Trust awards in 1999, cartoons are able to capture in one space what journalists have spent days researching, and ages talking about.

Savagery in Political Cartoons.

In addition to the question of impact, any study of British Election cartoons since 1945 naturally raises the question of savagery. Have political cartoons become more savage in their attacks on politicians during this period? Do these savage cartoons have a greater or lesser impact on the political scene? It is difficult to know whose definition of "savage" to use in such a discussion, but it is nevertheless clear that some cartoonists are pleased by the extent to which they offend "good taste". When Low worked on the *Evening Standard* in the 1930s he was no doubt pleased to be regarded as offensive and outrageous by Hitler and Mussolini, but rather more surprisingly Stanley Baldwin was of the same opinion. Arthur Christiansen, editor of the *Daily Express*, had lunch with Baldwin in 1935, and was left in no doubt as to his preference for Sidney Strube, the *Daily Express* cartoonist: "Strube is a gentle genius…I don't mind his attacks because he never hits below the belt. Now Low is a genius but he is evil and malicious. I cannot bear Low!" (*Headlines All My Life*, 1961, p.155.)

The definition of savagery is very subjective, but it is clear that after the prudish Victorian age, British political cartooning gradually regained its expressive and impassioned edge, particularly under the influence of cartoonists such as Will Dyson. By the end of the Second World War British cartoonists had also regained their liking for the personal attack. During the 1945 General Election campaign the political cartoonists certainly homed in on Harold Laski, and in the 1950 and 1951 General Elections they did their best to demonise Nye Bevan. Cummings - who had replaced Strube at the *Daily Express* - was a prominent member of this campaign, as he was of the later campaign to demonise Tony Benn.

It is doubtful whether many people nowadays would place Vicky in the category of a savage cartoonist, but in the 1950s and 1960s his personal attacks on Tory politicians like Macmillan certainly upset a lot of *Evening Standard* readers - or at least a lot of letter-writers - just as Low had done. The work of modern political cartoonists such as Scarfe (unfortunately not represented in this book), Steadman, Bell and Rowson should not blind us to the fact that their predecessors were also capable of savage and personal attacks. However, it would certainly be difficult to identify amongst current cartoonists someone sufficiently acceptable to the establishment as to follow Tenniel, Partridge, David Low and Osbert Lancaster in receiving a knighthood.

REFERENCES

All writers on post-war British politics owe a debt to the series of studies of British General Elections started by R.B. McCallum in 1947 with *The British General Election of 1945* (Oxford, OUP, 1947). Four years later H.G. Nicholas produced a similar study for the General Election of 1950, and since that time David Butler and various colleagues have written monographs on each British General Election. Since 1951 these have been published by Macmillan, and are based on research reports funded through Nuffield College, Oxford. In 1986, following a conference at Essex University, Cambridge University Press published *Communications: The General Election Campaign of 1983* (Cambridge, CUP, 1986). This series has continued with studies of the General Elections of 1987, 1992 and 1997, all of them co-edited by Ivor Crewe.

Timothy Benson, "Low and Beaverbrook", PhD Thesis, University of Kent at Canterbury, 1998.

Mark Bryant "Poison Pen or Good-Tempered Pencil? Humour and Hatred in 20th Century Political Cartoons", in Robert Edwards (ed) *A Sense of Permanence? Essays on the Art of the Cartoon* (Canterbury, University of Kent, 1997)

Mark Bryant, *Dictionary of Twentieth-Century British Cartoonists and Caricaturists* (London, Ashgate, 2000)

Arthur Christiansen, *Headlines All My Life* (London, Heinemann, 1961)

Stephen Glover, *Paper Dreams* (London, Jonathan Cape, 1993)

Roy Greenslade "I'm a Fig Leaf for Page 3", *Guardian*, 2 October 2000, "Media" p.2.

John Harvey "An Interview with Nicholas Garland", in Robert Edwards (ed) *A Sense of Permanence? Essays on the Art of the Cartoon* (Canterbury, University of Kent, 1997)

Derek Jameson, *Last of the Hot Metal Men: From Fleet Street to Showbiz* (London, Ebury Press, 1990)

Martin Rowson "We Are the *True* Outsiders of Journalism", *British Journalism Review*, Vol.12 No.1 (2001)

Gerald Scarfe, *Scarfe by Scarfe* (London, Hamish Hamilton, 1986)

Ralph Steadman "Ralph Steadman Introduces a Special Issue," *Observer Magazine*, 27 December 1992, p.7.

Colin Seymour-Ure, "Drawn and Quartered: The Election in Cartoons", in Ivor Crewe and Martin Harrop (eds) *Political Communications: The General Election Campaign of 1983* (Cambridge, CUP, 1986)

"Here you are!   Don't lose it again!"

Philip Zec's dramatic General Election cartoon "Here you are! Don't lose it again!" appeared in the Daily Mirror *of 4 July 1945, and summed up many people's feelings in the aftermath of war. Yet this was not in fact a new cartoon, as it had first appeared in the paper's "Victory in Europe Day" edition of 8 May 1945.*

Chapter 1

"Here You Are! Don't Lose it Again!"

"Love me, love my dog" by "Vicky" - Victor Weisz - was published in the News Chronicle *of 23 May 1945. It identifies the separation between Churchill and the Conservative Party - and also attempts less successfully to suggest that the Tory Party has in some sense eaten the Beveridge report.*

The Run-up to the 1945 General Election

The General Election of 1935 had seen the return of a National Government, containing Conservative, National Liberal, National Labour members. It was a continuation - or as some would see it a hangover - of the 1931 government with the same political title. The General Election which had been due in 1940 was prevented by the war.

The pre-war political climate had been set by large scale unemployment, particularly affecting what contemporaries called "the working classes", and accompanied paradoxically by increased prosperity amongst those who were actually in work. The National Government - first under Stanley Baldwin and then under Neville Chamberlain - had also been responsible for the policy of "Appeasement". This was an attempt to enable Adolf Hitler, the leader of Nazi Germany, to satisfy his territorial ambitions on Continental Europe, in order to avoid involving the United Kingdom in war. The policy failed and the United Kingdom felt itself obliged to go to war with Germany over Poland.

Military disasters in Norway forced the resignation of Chamberlain as Prime Minister in 1940. He was replaced by Winston Churchill, at that time regarded by many as a voluble politician of uncertain political adherence, who had nonetheless opposed the policy of Appeasement. A coalition of all parties was thought to be desirable to fight the war, and Churchill's government was extended to include the Labour Party and what still remained of an independent Liberal Party.

FAREWELL

"Since there's no help, come let us kiss and part."

*Ernest Shepard was not as powerful a political cartoonist as he
was an illustrator of Winnie the Pooh. However, his cartoon
"Farewell" in* Punch *of 30 May 1945 captures nicely the insincere
regrets of politicians at the resumption of party politics.*

"His Face is Their Fortune" by "Stephen" - Stephen Roth - from the Sunday Pictorial *of 3 June 1945, shows the attempt to hide the Tory Party behind Churchill's image.*

There was little overt political activity during the war. That is not to say that there was an absence of political discussion in the country, or even in the armed services, but the major parties had agreed not to fight against each other in by-elections. The major event of domestic policy was that Sir William Beveridge produced a report on National Insurance intended to try and defeat the enemies of unemployment, poverty and old age.

After the surrender of Germany in May 1945, Churchill wanted to continue leading the wartime government, probably until after the defeat of Japan. The Labour Party said no, so on 23 May Churchill resigned, formed the so-called "Caretaker" government - now consisting entirely of Conservatives, National Liberals and Nationals - and announced the General Election for 5 July.

Vicky's cartoon "Bow-Wow", from the News Chronicle *of 6 June 1945, shows Churchill barking to scare voters away from dummies of Morrison, Attlee and Bevin, which have been set up in Nazi uniform as Himmler, Hitler and Goering.*

DREAMLAND

David Low's "Dreamland" cartoon, published in the London Evening Standard *of 7 June 1945, refers satirically to Churchill's "Gestapo" broadcast. Nightmare might have been a more appropriate title, but Churchill apparently sleeps soundly alongside his advisers Brendan Bracken and Lord Beaverbrook.*

Composition of the House of Commons at the 1945 General Election

The party's strengths at the 1945 General Election were:

Conservative	361 seats
National Liberal	27 seats
National	9 seats
Labour	166 seats
Independent	20 seats
Other Parties	13 seats

Because of the political truce the composition of the House of Commons had not changed significantly since 1935. There had, however, been a number of Conservative losses in by-elections to "Commonwealth Party" candidates, who represented both a left-wing (though unofficial) version of the Labour Party, and the opinions of all those who wanted to oppose the Conservatives.

Leslie Illingworth's cartoon "Nocturne", from Punch *of 13 June 1945 shows a worried electorate listening to competing views conveyed through radio election broadcasts.*

NOCTURNE

THE DUMMY THAT WASN'T

Sidney Strube's cartoon "The Dummy That Wasn't", published in the Daily Express on 18 June 1945, tries to suggest that Attlee was subordinate to Harold Laski, with Ernest Bevin and Stafford Cripps standing in the wings. The reference on the placard is to Charlie McCarthy, dummy of popular American ventriloquist Edgar Bergen.

Herbert Morrison

Election Issues and the 1945 Campaign

The Labour Party launched a double-barrelled assault in the 1945 campaign. They harked back to the history of the 1930s - insecurity, unemployment, Appeasement and war - and at the same time projected an ideal vision of a future society which would give greater encouragement to a larger number of people. They proposed nationalisation of major industries and had a five year plan to draw together the resources of the nation. This second barrel was captured in the Labour slogan on its posters: "Let us face the future".

The Conservative and associated parties understandably had only a single barrel to fire, since they did not want to dwell on the public's unhappy memories of the 1930s. Their slogan was "Help him finish the job" - a specific reference both to the continuing war against Japan, and to the role of Winston Churchill as war leader. Electors were enjoined not to vote Conservative but still to vote "National", and the Labour Party was not pleased with the apparent suggestion that only the Conservatives were a national party.

Vicky's cartoon "The Big Three", from the News Chronicle of 26 June 1945, refers to the meeting of the "Big Three" - the United States, Soviet Union, and United Kingdom - at Potsdam, but transposes it to concerns about basic political issues. Churchill is once again shown with Brendan Bracken and Lord Beaverbrook.

The 1945 General Election was fought through public meetings - although rarely joint hustings; through loud-speaker vans with candidates touring the streets; and, significantly, through radio broadcasts. These latter occurred every night from 4 to 30 June 1945. Churchill - under the "National" slogan "Successful War Leader" - undertook four out of the ten Conservative broadcasts. As it turned out, this was not as beneficial to the fortunes of the Conservative Party as he and the planners had supposed.

The Big Three

5

FRANKENSTEIN

The Daily Mail *of 29 June 1945 carried Illingworth's cartoon
"Frankenstein", in which a nervous voter confronts the Frankenstein
monster of government that has been built by Attlee and Morrison.*

Churchill's first radio speech revealed his switch from war leader to politician. During this speech he accused the Labour Party of being bent on establishing a socialist system, despite the fact that the party was led by people such as Clement Attlee, Herbert Morrison, Ernest Bevin and Hugh Dalton who had served with him throughout his government. This might not in itself have seemed a terrible accusation for a party that still professed to be socialist, but Churchill extended his diatribe by claiming that a Labour Government would have to "fall back on some kind of Gestapo, no doubt very humanely directed in the first instance."

This extraordinary accusation, against people with whom Churchill had worked for five years, may well have rebounded on him, and it certainly became the subject of many cartoons. Attlee's response was characteristically mild and sad in tone: he said that in his travesty of Labour Policy, Churchill clearly "wanted the electors to understand how great was the difference between Winston Churchill, the great leader in war of a United Nation, and Mr Churchill the party leader of the Conservatives." Attlee also commented that "The voice we heard last night was that of Mr Churchill but the mind was that of Lord Beaverbrook." Both the Gestapo accusation and the reference to Lord Beaverbrook became the subject of cartoons, and may well have confirmed in the minds of many newspaper readers the ludicrous nature of Churchill's accusation.

"ST. GEORGE, THE STEED AWAITS!"

Low returned to the Laski issue for "St. George, the steed awaits!", his cartoon in the London Evening Standard *of 4 July 1945, where Churchill is shown offering the English patron saint a red herring to ride rather than a horse.*

DR. BALLOT : " THE BABY ARRIVED YESTERDAY, BUT WE CAN'T TELL YOU WHO
HE'LL TAKE AFTER, UNTIL THE 26TH."

Debate between Churchill and Attlee was also caused by the chairman of the Labour Party's National Executive Committee, Professor Harold Laski. While the result of the 1945 General Election was still undecided, Churchill invited Attlee to accompany him to a meeting of the "Big Three" in Potsdam. As Chairman of the NEC, Professor Laski declared that Attlee should reach no agreements at the meeting, since they could not be discussed in advance by the Parliamentary Labour Party and the NEC. Churchill and other Conservatives took this as the occasion for claiming that a Labour government would be subject to the dictates of extraparliamentary bodies, particularly the NEC and its chairman Laski.

This became the subject of many cartoons, although most of the electorate would not previously have heard of Professor Laski. It is interesting to note that Attlee never directly contradicted Laski, but contented himself with saying that there was no question of his going to Potsdam merely to observe, and that Churchill did not understand the Labour Party. It was in relation to a later outburst by Laski that Attlee gave him the high quality put-down: "Your letter has been received and its contents noted. A period of silence on your part would be most welcome."

Despite the Conservative by-election losses, and the public-opinion surveys showing a Labour lead, the national newspapers focused on the popularity of Churchill and forecast a Tory victory.

Strube's cartoon of "Dr. Ballot", in the Daily Express *of 6 July 1945, refers to the delay in producing the result of the General Election. As the votes of the British forces overseas could not be collected and counted immediately, Strube's "Little Man" is told that the British people will have to wait and see who has won.*

8

Lord Longford, then Frank Pakenham, remembers his 1945 Election contest with Conservative Candidate Quintin Hogg in Oxford City. Hogg had won the seat in a famous by-election in 1938, in a contest fought around his support of Chamberlain's surrender to Hitler at Munich: "The future Lord Hailsham was a formidable opponent. He was an old friend of Elizabeth (Longford's wife) and a brilliant contemporary of mine at Eton and Oxford (a double First and Fellowship of All Souls). But feelings ran high during the election. When he came to tea and Elizabeth offered him a second cup of tea my son Paddy, aged 8, refused to get up and bring it to him. Oxford was no doubt unwinnable at that time. I had been a Cowley councillor but Cowley and Headington were still excluded from the constituency. But nothing could spoil his triumph. It was thought rather ungenerous at the count where I said that 'the Conservatives had won Oxford for the last time.' I still think that I had the better policy but Quintin was the more effective candidate". It is difficult to imagine candidates entertaining each other to tea in 2001.

Personalities in the 1945 General Election

Winston Churchill

Winston Churchill was Prime Minister of the National Government, and Leader of the Conservative Party. He was a major political figure for forty years, first with the Conservatives, then with the Liberals, then with the Conservatives again. His opposition to Appeasement had been a minority view in the Conservative Party, attracting little support because people preferred to think of peace rather than the military requirements for creating it. Churchill's views on India and on the abdication of Edward VIII confirmed doubts about his political judgement. In 1945 a revered war leader, whose energy and dedication in the pursuit of victory - expressed through eloquent radio broadcasts - was believed to represent many of the best characteristics of the British people. As Churchill later put it, he "gave the lion's roar."

Clement Attlee

A minor figure in the Labour government of 1929-31, Clement Attlee succeeded to the leadership of the Labour Party in 1935, almost by accident. Its parliamentary destruction in 1931 had left the party with no major figures in the House of Commons - except George Lansbury whose pacifism was too much even for the Labour Party.

"CHEER UP! THEY WILL FORGET YOU BUT THEY WILL REMEMBER ME ALWAYS"

THE LEADER OF HUMANITY

As Churchill's deputy Prime Minister during the war, Attlee ran Cabinets and committees in a totally different way from Churchill, emphasising the efficient conduct of business rather than delivering eloquent speeches. Attlee was often thought of and often caricatured as a pygmy in relation to Churchill, who is said to have described him as "a modest little man with plenty to be modest about." The comparison between Attlee and Churchill was again thought to be cruel, as when his modest and rather boring speaking style was contrasted with the purple eloquence of Churchill.

The London Evening Standard of 31 July 1945 carried Low's "Two Churchills", dealing with the consequences of Election defeat. Here Low suggests that even in defeat Churchill will have monumental status, based on his reputation as a war leader.

Lord Beaverbrook

Lord Beaverbrook was a friend of Churchill, an off-and-on member of Churchill's war government, and a member of the Conservative Party - although often a critic of it. Perhaps even more significantly for this book, Beaverbrook was also owner of the *Express* group of newspapers, and of the London *Evening Standard* in which David Low's cartoons appeared. Beaverbrook had spent twenty years proclaiming that the political stance taken by Low was nothing to do with him, and at the time of the 1945 General Election he continued to support the publication of Low's increasingly pro-Labour and anti-Tory cartoons, apparently without any attempt to censor them.

Professor Harold Laski

A Professor, and a charismatic teacher at the London School of Economics, Harold Laski was deeply involved in Labour Party politics. Together with R.H. Tawney and G.D.H. Cole, Laski was one of three major theoreticians who contributed to the intellectual case for Socialism in a way that no academics have subsequently done. However, Laski also contributed a level of self-importance and political naiveté which made him an uncomfortable colleague, especially in his role as chairman of the Labour Party - an office that sounded more significant than it actually was.

The Results of the 1945 General Election

Because of the need to count the votes of the overseas forces, the result of the General Election was not announced until 26 July 1945. It showed a huge turnover between the Conservatives and their allies and the Labour Party, although as always the British Electoral system overemphasised the scale of the turnaround. The Conservatives and their allies lost 172 seats. The Labour Party gained 227 seats, and, characteristically, Attlee's diary entry for 26 July 1945 was "quite an exciting day".

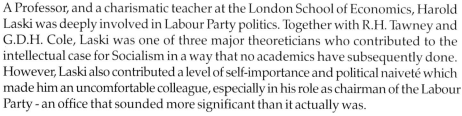

Labour	393	48.3%
Conservatives	213	39.8%
Liberal	12	9.1%
Others	22	2.7%

Looking back from the year 2001, it may seem strange that two Communists were elected.

Cartoonist of the 1945 General Election

Phillip Zec has been chosen as cartoonist of the 1945 Election, not for a sequence of significant images, but for a single dramatic cartoon in the *Daily Mirror* of 4 July 1945, entitled "Here you are! Don't lose it again!" This cartoon represents the themes that struck most potently during the Election, although it was not in fact a new cartoon, being reprinted from the *Daily Mirror* on "Victory in Europe Day", 8 May 1945.

Phillip Zec was appointed political cartoonist of the *Daily Mirror* in 1937, and achieved prominence in the history of political cartoons on 5 March 1942, when the paper carried his stark image of a torpedoed sailor on a raft over the caption "The Price of Petrol Has Been Increased by One Penny - Official". Zec's strong wartime style gradually diminished in effect, but it was still powerful in 1945. He remained with the *Daily Mirror* until 1954, and subsequently worked as political cartoonist on the *Daily Herald* from 1958 to 1961.

Chapter 2

Consolidation not Adventure.

THREE-LEGGED HANDICAP RACE

Illingworth's Daily Mail cartoon "Three-Legged Handicap Race" of 12 January 1950 shows Attlee labelled as Socialist, and burdened with the supposed losses of nationalised industries, whilst Churchill is handicapped by lies about him rather than by any Conservative failings. The Liberals, represented by their leader Clement Davies, are simply shown as not commanding enough support.

The Run-up to the 1950 General Election

Since 1945 the Labour government had carried through a legislative programme extraordinary in size, complexity and impact. Whole industries such as coal and rail were taken into public ownership through the process of "nationalisation", whilst the new National Health Service extended the provision of free health facilities from the most poor to everyone in society.

Following the wartime Beveridge Report, reforms to the National Insurance system were also carried through, providing for payment of benefits to those who were sick and unemployed. In later years Labour left-wingers would look back on these measures with pink-tinted spectacles, as a first major advance of Socialism - sadly from their point of view an advance that was subsequently lost.

These years also saw full employment, a phenomenon which Labour sought to emphasise as a distinguishing characteristic between itself and the Conservative Party. An extraordinary feature of the period before the 1950 General Election was that Labour did not lose one of its own seats in by-elections, and yet this first Labour Government with a full majority was obliged to work within a difficult economic environment - the consequence of devoting all Britain's resources to fighting the war.

Labour's emphasis on "fair shares", though initially popular, existed within an extremely difficult economic context. The relationship between the pound and the dollar became so unrealistic that Stafford Cripps, the Chancellor of the Exchequer, was forced into a devaluation of the pound against the dollar. There were shortages of almost everything, and, through the continuation of wartime rationing, coupons or points were required for purchasing many things especially clothing and food. Aid supplied by the United States through the "Marshall Plan" provided immediate help, but left open the question of what would happen when it ended.

The Conservative Party naturally seized on government problems and turned them into government failures. They hammered away at the facts of shortages, rationing and controls as unpopular aspects of the way in which the British were required to live. However, they also showed their ability to recognise a political good thing when they saw it, and proclaimed their adherence to the major elements of the Welfare State and to the continuation of full employment. Rab Butler led this renewal of Conservative policy, while Churchill focused on writing his history of the Second World War, with occasional excursions into painting and equally occasional appearances in the political arena.

Leslie Illingworth's cartoon "The Voter in Wonderland", from Punch *of 18 January 1950, refers to the episode in Lewis Carroll's* Through the Looking Glass *where Alice finds Tweedledum and Tweedledee having a fierce but inconsequential argument.*

THE VOTER IN WONDERLAND

I. OPTIMISM AND PESSIMISM

" I'm a political cartoonist, doctor, and the election has already induced a very disquieting little neurosis "

Cummings himself appears in an unusually jokey cartoon from the Daily Express of 21 January 1950, published under the headline "It's getting on top of me...says Cummings." Attlee, Bevin, Churchill and Bevan are all recognisable in the furniture of the analyst's room, where one of the door knobs has the face of Manny Shinwell, Lord Woolton is the barometer, and Anthony Eden supports Bevin - at least for the purposes of the cartoon. Strachey and Rab Butler also appear, and the large face in the chair under Churchill is a composite figure that Cummings frequently used to represent his nightmares of the Labour Party - "Zilly Boy Shinbag".

In foreign policy there was increasing unhappiness with the influence of the Soviet Union on the eastern European countries which had fallen within its orbit. This led to a feeling of insecurity which in turn led to the creation of the North Atlantic Treaty Organisation, designed to give defence against an expansionist Soviet Union. This development of foreign policy was not a matter of dispute between the political parties, although there were some rumblings against it within Labour.

Election Issues and the 1950 Campaign

On 10 January 1950 the General Election was announced for 23 February - a timing which looks even more extraordinary now than it did then. Instead of holding on until the Spring, Attlee had decided to call an early General Election, in the belief that constant discussion of when it might be held was getting in the way of industrial production. It was also felt that Labour had carried through the programme on which it had been elected, and therefore required a new mandate.

However, for most people at the time the new mandate it sought did not seem especially exciting. In a campaign led by Herbert Morrison, who, with Bevin and Cripps, was one of the three great figures that circled around Attlee, Labour projected itself as seeking "consolidation". It also threw in some relatively random proposals for further nationalisation of cement, industrial assurance, sugar and water supplies. The sugar interests, led by Tate and Lyle, responded with a vigorous poster campaign before the General Election, including images of "Mr Cube" waving a sword representing free enterprise.

The Labour case was essentially one of asking to be re-elected on the grounds that they had done good things for most people. Their manifesto was entitled "Let Us Win Through Together", as against the Tory manifesto "This Is The Road". Throughout the Election the Conservative Party

continued to hammer away at shortages - with the resulting rationing and controls - at extravagance and at nationalisation. They pledged to continue full employment and effective social services, and would stop further nationalisation - although having no proposals to return coal and rail to private ownership. More familiarly to us now, the Conservative Party also proposed to release enterprise, and to cut both government spending and taxation.

During the campaign additional issues emerged, including a dispute over whether it would be possible to increase the petrol ration, whether it was desirable to set up high-level talks with the Soviet Union - as Churchill wanted, and, in a brief burst of Churchill's old rhetoric, whether the Labour government wanted to impose state ownership and employment on every aspect of life.

Low's London Evening Standard *cartoon of 27 January 1950 - "This is the Road" - is particularly interesting. It illustrates a continuing problem for the postwar Conservative Party in promising both tax cuts and an improved welfare state. The car contains Lord Woolton on the left, and on the right - almost crushed beneath Churchill - Rab Butler. As an extra joke there is a commentary from Low's famous Colonel Blimp character, sitting on the fence and talking to Low himself.*

In the Daily Herald *of 3 February 1950 Low drew Churchill and Woolton turning their backs on the reality of economic development since the war, and urging voters to "Walk up! Walk up! See the 'Failure of Socialism'".*

Nye Bevan's success as Minister of Health apparently failed to overcome doubts about his aggressive language, and he was not given a very prominent role in Labour's Election campaign of 1950. David Ghilchik's cartoon in Time and Tide *of 4 February 1950 compares his gagged inability to repeat his comments about Tory "vermin" with Herbert Morrison's siren song wooing the floating voter.*

A more parochial dispute, referred to in several of the cartoons included here, arose from the use of the title "Liberal". There had been National Liberals in the previous Election campaign, but the Independent Liberal Party had survived the 1945 General Election, and in 1950 it objected strongly to the inclusion of "Liberal" in the title used by some candidates. Its claim was that National Liberals were really just Conservatives hiding away under a different name, and various inclusions of the word Liberal with Conservative were cited.

The most extreme example was that of Doctor Charles Hill, who described himself as Liberal-Conservative, and explicitly claimed that he was different from a National Liberal. Hill was a significant figure in terms of his public visibility during the 1950 Election campaign. Previously a vehement leader of the doctors opposed to the National Health Service, Hill used his reputation and familiar style to support the Conservatives in this Election. A deep fruity voice gave individuality to his pungent phrases and folksy delivery - as a radio doctor, he had once referred to "the prune, that black coated worker" as a way of tackling the problems of constipation.

The Liberals created some visibility for themselves by attacking the unauthorised use of their name, but otherwise had difficulty in establishing their position in relation to the other two parties. Radio, along with national newspapers, continued to provide the main focus for election issues, as television viewing continued to be very much a minority activity. Churchill did not repeat the claimed errors of his radio campaign of 1945, and indeed took only one of the Conservative's five broadcasts. Nonetheless he achieved a 51% listenership for this broadcast, compared to 44% for Attlee's most listened-to broadcast.

The contrast between Attlee and Churchill remained as evident as in the 1945 General Election campaign. The electorate was now more familiar with Attlee's understated, laconic and - to many people - unimpressive style of speaking. Churchill remained the great public speaker and successful war leader, and, as in the 1945 campaign, he received cries of "Good old Winnie" from people who subsequently disappeared to vote Labour. In those more deferential days little if any mention was made of his age - seventy-five.

The 1950 General Election was fought with little hyperbole. The few examples of supposedly personal abuse would now strike us as being very mild, although people did recall the more heightened language used by Aneurin - commonly called Nye - Bevan. Two years before the campaign he had admitted his burning hatred for the Tory Party, and said that "so far as I am concerned they are lower than vermin". Since Bevan also described the British press as "the most prostituted in the world" it is not surprising that the newspapers made him into a target.

Rodger's cartoon in The People *of 12 February 1950 shows Churchill offering the Liberal voter a very uncomfortable seat on the back of his tandem, while Mr Cube from the Tate and Lyle anti-nationalisation campaign tries to hold Attlee back.*

Election Personalities

Ernest Bevin

Ernie Bevin was born illegitimate and received no formal education after the age of eleven. He became a Trade Union leader, first with the dockers, and later within the successive amalgamations that led to the creation of the huge Transport and General Workers Union - of which he was the first General Secretary in 1922. While his first priority was the Union, and fighting for better conditions as the "Dockers KC", Bevin became more prominent in Labour politics from 1930 onwards. His position was secured both as holder of his Trade Union "block vote" at Labour Party conferences, and also by a large if sometimes overbearing personality. Bevin made a very bad enemy.

Churchill remained a great supporter of the term "Liberal", but Vicky's cartoon "The Dance of the Seven Veils", in the News Chronicle *of 21 February 1950, suggests it is inadequate cover for Conservatism.*

THE DANCE OF THE SEVEN VEILS

8 MORE DAYS BEFORE YOU GO TO VOTE

3-point Election Notebook

Cartoon by Cummings

". . . And above all, let COOL REASON, not emotion, guide you in the General Election."

Michael Cummings' cartoon in the Daily Express *of 15 February 1950 does allow Bevan a voice, and highlights the emotion contained in - and aroused by - his speeches. Morrison, Attlee and Cripps sit on Bevan's right, while to his left - at least in terms of the cartoon - sit Ernest Bevin and Manny Shinwell, a leading figure in the Labour Party.*

In 1940, at the age of fifty-nine, Bevin entered the House of Commons, and acquired a wholly new reputation as Minister of Labour under Churchill. That role seemed to make him an obvious candidate for Chancellor of the Exchequer, but in 1945 Attlee gave him the post of Foreign Secretary. Here Bevin was quick to identify a potential threat from Soviet Russia, and to participate in the creation of NATO to counter it. His forceful adoption of that position, and his inability - shared with many others - to deal successfully with the problems of Jews and Arabs in Palestine, led to trouble within the Labour Party.

Bevin expressed his anger over this criticism in a famous remark about being "stabbed in the back", a phrase that was subsequently adopted for a collection of Vicky cartoons, and which inspired the title of this book. Bevin was not an orator, being harsh-voiced and relatively clumsy in expression, but he was a hugely important man, and a loyal supporter of the much lesser Attlee. He was much admired by the mandarins in the Foreign Office.

Herbert Morrison

A conscientious objector during the First World War, Herbert Morrison became an MP and a senior member of the Labour Government of 1929. Morrison lost his seat in 1931, but he maintained his reputation as a politician through his management of the London County Council. Morrison's importance to the Labour Party was increased when it adopted his view of the structure appropriate to a nationalised industry – not directed by Socialist principles but run as a centralised bureaucracy.

Morrison would almost certainly have been leader of the Labour Party if he had not lost his seat in 1931. When he returned to Parliament after the General Election of 1935 he found himself unable to displace Attlee. Ernest Bevin in particular was always protective of Attlee against those who wished to push either Cripps or Morrison into the PM's job. Denied the chance of running a major department, Morrison gave his energies after 1945 to a general overview of the Government's business, and led the pressure to opt for "consolidation" in the General Election of 1950.

Lord Woolton

Fred Woolton was never an MP, but had been given governmental responsibility by Churchill during the war. A successful business man, and a particularly successful salesman, Lord Woolton was one of those almost non-political figures which the Conservative Party of the time liked to present as its public face. As Chairman of the Conservative Party he brought what was seen as smooth efficiency to the projection of the party, and his rubicund face and bristly eyebrows helped to sustain a non-threatening image.

The Results of the 1950 General Election

The number of constituencies had been cut down from 640 to 625. The 84% turnout was larger than in any prewar General Election, and has not been achieved since. The results and percentages were as follows.

Labour	315	46.1%
Conservative and Allies	298	43.4%
Liberals	9	9.2%
Other	2	1.3%

The Communists put up 100 candidates, but acquired only 0.3% of the vote and lost their seats, the highest share of the poll in any seat being 21%. The Speaker - a Conservative - was unopposed.

The Cartoonist of the 1950 General Election

During the 1950 General Election David Low moved from the London *Evening Standard* to the *Daily Herald* - in other words, from being independently critical of the Conservatives in a Conservative paper, to working for a newspaper that openly supported the Labour Party. Low had been born in New Zealand, and had first made his reputation in Australia before joining the London *Star* in 1919. Low had moved to Lord Beaverbrook's *Evening Standard* in 1927, but his proprietor's willingness to stir up trouble even amongst his friends found expression in a contract which apparently gave Low complete freedom in drawing his cartoons.

SUBCONSCIOUS UNEASINESS CAUSED BY MEETING ONE'S OWN WAXWORK.

Later research has demonstrated that in fact not all his cartoons were accepted by the paper, but Low provided enduring images of the Coalition ass, the TUC carthorse and Colonel Blimp. His cartoons of Lloyd George, Churchill and Beaverbrook seem much less critical than his successors of today would produce, as he focused on their policies and did not ridicule them in personal terms. Even his cartoons of Hitler and Mussolini did not portray physically - repellent dictators.

Low's transfer from the *Standard* to the *Daily Herald* was followed in 1953 by his final move to what was then the *Manchester Guardian*. In 1962 Low was knighted, a distinction previously bestowed on cartoonists such as John Tenniel, Bernard Partridge and Leslie Ward, but unlikely to be offered to - or accepted by - their most prominent modern successors.

Chapter 3
The Grand Old Man Returns.

"FINE, BOYS—THAT'LL GET THEM."

Leslie Illingworth's cartoon "Fine, boys - that'll get them", from Punch *of 19 September 1951, focuses on one of the significant campaign themes - Churchill as a supposed warmonger. Attlee is shown gleefully encouraging Shinwell and Morrison as they focus the projector and adjust the Churchill figure. Shinwell, as Minister of Defence, was at the fore in accusing Churchill of warmongering.*

"PUSSY, PUSSY — TO HEEL!"

In "Pussy, Pussy - to Heel!" in the News Chronicle of 20 September 1951, Bevan was drawn by Vicky with a surprising lack of sympathy. The Bevanites had published a pamphlet entitled "Going my way", outlining their beliefs of how Labour should proceed. Here Bevan and an almost unrecognisable Harold Wilson are depicted as lions escaping from a circus run by Morgan Phillips, Secretary of the Labour Party. In the background Gaitskell and John Strachey are rushing either to support Phillips or attack Bevan – although there was little difference between these actions.

The Run-up to the 1951 General Election

The Election of 1950 left the Labour Party with a majority of only six, but it never lost a vote in the House of Commons on a big issue. Given this small majority the further nationalisation of sugar, cement and assurance proposed in the 1950 manifesto were not carried through, although the reorganisation of the iron and steel industry enacted in 1949 was implemented.

Two senior Cabinet Ministers - Cripps and Bevin - died during the parliament. The replacement of Cripps as Chancellor by Hugh Gaitskell - a younger public-school educated lecturer, and of Bevin as Foreign Secretary by Herbert Morrison, had massive short and long-term consequences. Nye Bevan was not given either job.

Morrison's discomfort in his new role as Foreign Secretary was obvious, and Attlee said his acceptance of the job was "rather bad luck on him as it turned out". Gaitskell attempted to provide a massive rearmament programme to support British involvement in the Korean War by implementing charges in the previously free National Health Service.

Bevan, infuriated by the charges in "his" NHS, and objecting to the unreality of the defence expenditure, resigned from the government. He was accompanied by one Cabinet Minister, Harold Wilson, and a junior Minister John Freeman.

By the time of the 1951 General Election the Labour government was facing increasing economic problems with the dollar shortage, and had suffered a major crisis in foreign affairs when Iran - then known as Persia - pushed out British interests in the oil industry. Bevan and his followers had also created a Bevanite group within the Labour Party, and the Conservative

On 25 September 1951 David Low, now with the Daily Herald, illustrated his belief that the Conservatives had no policies. In "You can't blame them for keeping it dark," Beaverbrook, Woolton and Eden are shown on the left, trying to conceal the sack holding Conservative party policy. On the right Maxwell Fyfe - a leading Tory lawyer - is shown with a relatively benign Churchill, who is attempting to stop the young David Eccles from speaking out.

YOU CAN'T BLAME THEM FOR KEEPING IT DARK

At least the cause of party unity will spare us...

... those devastating cannonades from the Left

...those inflammatory speeches.

. . . the deafening thunder of dropped bricks.

"M⁺ ATTLEE IS THE MOST DYNAMIC, COLOURFUL AND ALL-KNOWING P.M. SINCE M⁺ GLADSTONE..."

BEVAN-PROOF SHELTER

—BUT INSTEAD . . . just constructive speeches.

But after Election Day.

On 25 September 1951, Cummings in the Daily Express *portrayed Attlee attempting to muzzle Nye Bevan during the Election campaign. As always, when Attlee was drawn with other people he appeared as a pygmy-like figure, but it also suited Conservative propaganda to portray Bevan as a much larger and therefore a much more significant figure. Attlee, Morrison and Gaitskell huddle in the "Bevan-Proof Shelter" presumed to be necessary after the Election*

Party found itself facing a government which looked old, tired and split. Even Churchill at seventy-seven looked younger than many of the senior figures in the Labour Cabinet.

The Conservative Party was thus in the happy position of being able to criticise the Labour government, and to portray Bevan as a wild left-winger about to take over the Labour Party, without having to promote any new ideas of its own. It is not clear what the balance was in Attlee's mind between exhaustion and genuine concern for national welfare, but on 19 September he announced a General Election for 25 October 1951.

Election Issues and the 1951 Campaign

The Conservative Party continued to hammer government extravagance, expensive and inefficient nationalisation, and what it said was Labour's doctrine of class war. Their manifesto promised to halt nationalisation, but - with the exception of iron and steel - did not propose that nationalised industries should revert to private ownership. At its national conference the Conservative Party had been bounced into promising to build 300,000 houses, and managed to turn a conference defeat into a major election proposal.

The Labour manifesto did not propose major new legislation, but continued the "consolidation" theme of 1950. It talked about social equality and the desirability of price controls, and emphasised the Labour government's contribution to peace, employment and a 50% increase in output compared with the years before the war. The proposed nationalisations in the 1950 manifesto quietly disappeared.

"ANYTHING YOU CAN DO, I CAN DO BETTER..."

These themes were reiterated in campaign speeches around the country, in radio broadcasts and in newspaper comment. Labour emphasised what it described as its achievements since 1945 especially on full employment and welfare, whilst Conservative speakers and writers emphasised nationalisation, bureaucracy and the cost of living. Yet the Election was conducted in what was considered a decorous fashion. Bevan and his followers gave no further ammunition to Conservatives, and much less was made of the split in the Labour Party than would probably have been the case fifty years later.

On 2 October 1951, Vicky in the News Chronicle *satirised the willingness of Churchill to compete with Labour on promises. "Anything you can do, I can do better" was an Irving Berlin song from the musical "Annie Get Your Gun", and Attlee appears here as Annie Oakley, whilst Churchill competes with him as sharpshooter Frank Butler. The promise of 300,000 houses was clearly relevant to more people than issues of capital gains and excess profit taxes.*

JON's cartoon "I'll woo him with these flowers..." in the Daily Graphic *of 9 October 1951 gives a different view of the likely impact of a continued Labour government. Attlee waits to present a bouquet to the middle class voter, whilst Morrison, Shinwell, Gaitskell and Bevan are portrayed with cudgels showing the real Labour intentions, and a smiling Hugh Dalton, the ex-Chancellor of the Exchequer, stands in the background. Shinwell and Bevan's attacks on Conservatives – a tinker's cuss and vermin – are repeated.*

"I'll woo him with these flowers, then you use the cudgels."

Cummings created "Mr Rising Price" as a dramatic representation of one of the themes of the 1951 Election campaign - the increasing cost of living. This editorial cartoon from the Daily Express *of 16 October 1951 shows Mr Rising Price in his most elongated form, being hurriedly pasted over with denials by Attlee and Gaitskell. "Mr Rising Price" was obviously designed to resemble the popular perception of a bureaucrat, with a stiff collar, a supercilious look, and a nose designed to stick into other people's business.*

"Wouldn't it be wonderful, Clem, if Mr. Rising Price was only an Express' stunt?"

The dispute over Persia became an election issue, since Churchill led the Conservative Party towards an aggressive response. The Labour Party had no problem in changing from criticising the Conservatives as the promoters of Appeasement before the war, to accusing them as the party most likely to lead the country into war. As the threat of the H-Bomb loomed in people's minds, the *Daily Mirror* tried to identify the Labour Government as more likely to sustain peace with the headline "Whose finger on the trigger?"

Radio was once again a major arena for electioneering. In the 1951 campaign Churchill and Charles Hill again attracted the highest proportion of listeners, although Churchill only broadcast once compared with his dominant four broadcasts in 1945. One of Charles Hill's broadcasts memorably christened Nye Bevan "the Tito of Tonypandy". The introduction of television broadcasts is historically important, but since they reached only 10% of the electorate in 1951, compared with 82% who listened at least once to the radio, it is unlikely they had any significant impact.

The 1951 Election campaign was also assisted by an increasing amount of information from public opinion polls, but with no contribution in terms of real news content from the BBC, whose news department continued to eschew any kind of political comment.

Personalities of the 1951 General Election

Aneurin (Nye) Bevan

Nye Bevan became a young Labour MP in 1929, and over the following decade was prominent as a left-winger often at odds with the formal Labour Party leadership. After 1940 he was one of the few people prepared to question Churchill's direction of the war, and Churchill described him as a "squalid nuisance". In 1945 Bevan was given responsibility for the Ministry of Health, which then also embraced housing. He thus presided over the introduction of the National Health Service and the attempt to rebuild British cities, and was thought by many to be a surprising success.

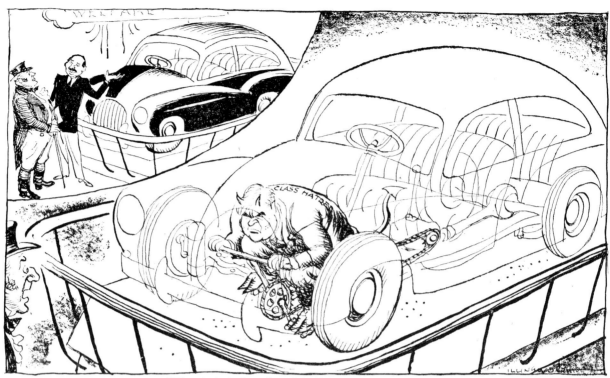

With apologies to the makers of the X-Ray Car at the Motor Show.

Unlike many Labour predecessors and successors, office did little to temper Bevan's views. His ability to offend the Conservative opposition was matched by his inability to remain on amicable terms with his Labour colleagues. It is said that Ernest Bevin, Labour's Foreign Secretary, was once told that "of course Nye is his own worst enemy". Bevin's reply was "not while I am alive he aint." (An alternative version has Morrison as the target.)

In 1951 Bevan resigned over changes in the NHS and rearmament, but he remained a volcanic presence with a group of adherents. In 1955 he was beaten by Gaitskell to the leadership of the Labour Party, and by 1959 was no longer a left wing bogey.

Stafford Cripps

Stafford Cripps was a middle-class, public school educated and relatively rich barrister, whose experiences in the 1930s turned him into a left winger. Cripps was elected to parliament in 1931, but like Bevan he remained at odds with his own leadership, particularly over the creation of a Popular Front against Naziism, and in 1939 he and Bevan were expelled from the Labour Party.

In the Daily Mail *of 18 October 1951 Leslie Illingworth gave his view of labour's promises. The Earls Court Motor Show had just opened, and in "B in the Bonnet" Illingworth shows his view of what existed under the bonnet of the smart new car that Attlee was offering John Bull - a scowling and demonic Bevan labelled with class hatred.*

ANYONE CAN SEE THAT THE CLOAK OF LIBERALISM HAS FALLEN ON US

In Vicky's News Chronicle *cartoon of 24 October 1951, "Anyone can see that the cloak of Liberalism has fallen on us", he returns to the issue of how far the Conservatives now represented the Liberal tradition. Churchill remained keen to absorb his former party, and of the six Liberal MPs returned at the 1951 Election, five had no Conservative opposition in their constituency. Here Woolton, Churchill, Beaverbrook, Eden, Brendan Bracken and Maxwell Fyfe are all shown with Lloyd George's hair, cloak and tweed suit.*

Cartoonists frequently presented Churchill as much larger than his political opponents. This cartoon by "JON" - William John Philpin Jones - in the Daily Graphic *of 23 October 1951 shows his opponents - including Attlee, Bevan, Shinwell, Morrison and Strachey - as small, childlike and ineffectual.*

Restored to favour during the war, Cripps was sent by Churchill on missions to Russia and India. Cripps was a vegetarian, a teetotaller and a devout Christian, and his self-belief was such that Churchill once commented, as Cripps walked through the House of Commons, "There but for the grace of God goes God".

Cripps was made Chancellor of the Exchequer in 1947, and his personal austerity of spirit and behaviour fitted well the austere economic times. In great contrast to his predecessor - the loud voiced and ebullient Hugh Dalton - Cripps was not widely attacked by cartoonists.

The Results of the 1951 General Election

The 1951 General Election saw a reduced turnout in safe seats, and the result was an 82.5% poll compared with 84% in 1950. However, both parties got more votes than in previous General Elections, and Labour's total of almost 14 million has never been exceeded. The outcome was a small but remarkably uniform swing to the Tories, and the specific results were:

Conservatives	321	48%
Labour	295	48.8%
Liberal	6	2.5%
Irish Nationalists	3	0.7%

The Cartoonist of the 1951 General Election

Michael Cummings started as a cartoonist in 1939 on the left wing weekly *Tribune*, and in 1948 he became the paper's political cartoonist. In the following year he joined Beaverbrook's *Daily Express*, and for the 1951 General Election campaign he created a major new cartoon figure - "Mr Rising Price". Through this Cummings splendidly illustrated one of the Conservative themes, and the figure grew quite literally from its early portrayal.

Cummings worked for the *Daily Express* from 1949 to 1990, but from 1958 to 1996 he also provided cartoons for the *Sunday Express*. In his later years he also drew for the *Daily Mail* and *The Times*, and small cartoons of activities in Parliament for *Punch*. Cummings had a very strong line in both senses of the word. His criticism was most savagely applied to the Labour Party, though he was not wholly averse to attacking the Conservatives - albeit more mildly. People who believe Scarfe, Steadman, Rowson and Bell to be especially savage should look at Cummings.

Chapter 4
The Crown Prince Takes Over.

POLITICAL CUP-TIE

Illingworth's "Political Cup-Tie" from Punch *of 20 April 1955 shows the start of the Election as two football teams running onto the pitch - although the supporters were as it turned out rather less enthusiastic than here. Eden leads the Conservatives, followed by Butler, Macmillan, and Doctor Charles Hill. Attlee leads out a surprisingly pugnacious Morrison - complete with an indication that he was blind in one eye, a characteristically sharp-faced Gaitskell, a gloomy-looking Chuter Ede and John Strachey. Bevan is bizarrely shown not as a member of the team, but as its trainer - or perhaps not bizarrely if you took a Conservative view of his strength within the Labour Party.*

Attlee was often drawn by cartoonists as a small man, and Illingworth's Daily Mail *cartoon of 4 May 1955 - "Talking Big" - shows him standing on the shoulders of Gaitskell, who in turn is supported by Bevan whilst Morrison props them all up. Bevan's position at the bottom of the pile may explain his scowl.*

Vicky's cartoon "Personal Announcements", in the Daily Mirror *of 22 April 1955, welcomed the attack by Gaitskell, Labour's Shadow Chancellor, on Butler's budget, which he saw both as inflationary and as favouring the richest people through tax reductions. The attack put paid to claims of "Butskellism."*

The Run-up to the 1955 General Election

After the Conservative Election victory in 1951, Churchill made an attempt to change the public perception of him as a class warrior, and appointed the conciliatory Sir Walter Monckton as Minister of Labour. Anthony Eden was naturally appointed as Foreign Secretary, whilst Rab Butler less predictably became Chancellor of the Exchequer. Over the next few years the underlying question of when Churchill would retire and hand on to Eden grew, and tension was especially strong in 1954, but there were still no major public disputes between senior members of the government.

Both Churchill and Eden had serious illnesses, but, in those less intrusive days, the newspapers did not focus upon this factor.

Britain was already involved in the war in Korea, but Eden's diplomatic skills had helped to avoid similar confrontation in Vietnam, and there were no significant party clashes over either conflict. The Labour front bench gave its support to Britain's own H-bomb, when that project was publicly announced, and the end of the occupation of

Disunity in the Labour Party was a major theme in the Election campaign, and this is represented particularly violently in Sidney Moon's cartoon "...and you'll find us one big happy family!" in the Sunday Dispatch *of 1 May 1955. Here Lady Megan Lloyd George is joining Labour from the Liberals, only to find that Attlee is carrying a broken billiard cue, Bevan and Morrison are fighting, and Labour MP Bessie Bradock has just hurled a bowl at the Party leader.*

'...AND YOU'LL FIND US ONE BIG HAPPY FAMILY!'

Illingworth's cartoon "Bevatskell", from the Daily Mail *of 22 April 1955, focuses on division at the head of the Labour Party, with Bevan drawn appropriately on the left and Gaitskell on the right of Attlee. The use of Bevan's name as the start of the compound name was probably deliberate, since the Conservatives viewed him as leader in waiting. There may also be a reference to the Economist's "Mr Butskell", a composite representing the supposed similarity of economic policy between Butler and Gaitskell.*

OPERATION OLIVE BRANCH

Cumming's cartoon "Operation Olive Branch...", in the Daily Express *of 11 May 1955, highlights the lack of dispute over foreign affairs in the 1955 campaign. Eden and Macmillan ride a rather implausible Conservative Dove of Peace, whilst Attlee, Morrison, Bevan and Morgan Phillips - General Secretary of the Labour Party - look for a way of destroying the illusion.*

"Now we've got to make them look like two war-mongers on a hydrogen bomber, with their fingers on the trigger."

Vicky's cartoon in the Daily Mirror *of 11 May 1955 - "He says we can double our standard of living in 25 years..." - refers to a view expressed by Rab Butler. The cartoon shows Vicky's two contrasting styles in a single cartoon, with the pinstriped Conservative in his usual cartoon style, and the two dubious pensioners more strongly drawn in what was called his "Oxfam" style.*

Germany on 5 May 1955 also failed to become a party issue. There were serious debates about the re-arming of Germany to meet the perceived threat from the Soviet Union, but the most significant clashes on this issue were within the Labour Party itself.

On the opposition benches there was still a noticeable split between the Labour leadership and Bevan and his followers. This had originally opened up over the National Health Service and rearmament, but it now continued with disputes not only about German rearmament but also about British policy in Asia. Bevan remained massively popular amongst Labour constituency members, but in the House of Commons he lost the deputy leadership election to Herbert Morrison, and he also lost to Hugh Gaitskell for the largely symbolic post of Treasurer of the Labour Party. The disunity of Labour, a significant feature of the coming election, was emphasised when a red-faced Bevan publicly disputed a statement by Attlee in the House of Commons, subsequently losing the party whip and only retaining membership of the Labour Party by one vote.

The Conservative Government presided over a growing economy, and naturally attracted the credit for it. Butler's immediate pre-election Budget provided a tax cut equal to 2.5p in the pound, and contemporaries regarded him as a very successful Chancellor - at least until some of his chickens came home

"He says we can double our standard of living in 25 years..."

to roost after the election. The Conservative Government did not undertake a major legislative programme, but the Minister of Housing, Harold Macmillan, kept its promise to build 300,000 houses, and it is interesting to note that four out of five of these were in the public sector. Butler deputised as Prime Minister when both Eden and Churchill were ill, but there was no question that Eden would succeed Churchill. The day of resignation finally occurred on 6 April 1955 which, sadly for Churchill, was during a newspaper strike. The General Election was set for 26 May.

Election Issues and the 1955 Campaign

The 1955 campaign contained few issues of major significance, and this was described as the dullest Election of the twentieth century. The Tory Government proclaimed the success it had achieved by building houses, and by not interfering with the economy. The Labour Party continued to emphasise peace as its major purpose, but could produce no equivalent to the warmongering scare of the 1951 Election campaign. Its manifesto offered a few pieces of nationalisation of no great significance, and talked about remedying social inequality, although it offered no clear view of how this might be achieved - except through the introduction of comprehensive schools.

Previous Labour Election campaigns had relied on portraying how awful Conservative dominated governments had been before the war, and on the possibility of disastrous changes of policy by future Conservative governments. Yet in the 1955 campaign the Tories could point to a successful

Cummings AND THE SOCIALISTS' ELECTION POSTER...

YOU CAN TRUST MR. ATTLEE

In the Daily Express *of 16 May 1955, Cummings adapts the Labour Party poster "You can trust Mr Attlee" to portray what was supposedly happening behind Attlee's friendly face.*

THE HISTORIC PARTY OF POWER, PELF & PRIVILEGE

Just let us get a nice REAL majority - that's all!

THE FLOATING VOTE

TORY PRESS

Our Liberal Inheritance

"IT'S NOT YOU SO MUCH, FAUNTLEROY, IT'S YOUR AWFUL GANG"

In 1953 Low had moved from the Daily Herald *to what was still called the* Manchester Guardian. *His cartoon "It's not* you *so much, Fauntleroy..." of 17 May 1955 represents Eden and Butler holding the Liberal inheritance of which the* Guardian *was still a part. Low himself is a literal floating voter, while in the background the crowd of Conservative supporters includes such unattractive figures as a teddy boy waving a cosh. Even readers of the* Guardian *might have had trouble understanding the word "Pelf" on their banner - it was a derogatory term for money.*

"WE ARE ALL WORKING CLASS NOW" – SIR DAVID ECCLES

LABOUR'S "CLOTHES: WELFARE STATE" etc. etc...

T.U. CARD

Vicky

" 'COURSE WE'VE CHANGED ! CAN'T YER SEE ? "

Vicky's cartoon "'Course we've changed..." in the Daily Mirror *of 24 May 1955 refers to a speech by Sir David Eccles, a middle-ranking Tory Minister. Eccles had claimed "We are all working class now", paraphrasing Sir William Harcourt's famous claim of sixty years earlier "We are all socialists now". Eccles appears on the far right next to Woolton, Butler, Eden and Macmillan. Churchill's credentials as a worker were more substantial, for - as shown in the picture on the wall - he did help build walls at his Chartwell home.*

economic record, a war in Korea which the previous Labour administration had supported, and a record of success on the economic front which had not been achieved through massive unemployment, or through cuts in social provision. The 1955 General Election was also the first since the ending of consumer rationing, as petrol, food and clothes had all successively been placed on the free market. The Tories tried a small scare by implying that a Labour government would bring rationing back, but Attlee in particular firmly rejected this suggestion.

The 1955 Election was really very quiet, with none of the robustness exemplified in previous election exchanges between Churchill and Attlee. It was one of many elections where the issue of disunity was thought to be a major feature in the success of the party that was not disunited. Bevan tried to play down elements of disunity within the Labour Party, which he himself exemplified, but although his choice of language was memorable it was not always particularly helpful to his own side. He appeared at one point to refer to the Tories as "Gadarene swine" and to claim that Christianity and Toryism were incompatible.

Churchill stirred up the campaign when he finally entered it, but Eden and Attlee retained a studied position of moderation in all things. This was Attlee's last Election as leader of his party. His understated style of reason and moderation gave force to Churchill's claim that he was "a

'Sssh! Let's hope he doesn't wake up in time...'

The 1955 Election campaign was so low key and lacking in excitement that the Labour-supporting Vicky worried about a low turnout of Labour voters. His cartoon "Sssh!..." in the Daily Mirror of 26 May 1955 suggests that Butler, Macmillan and Eden were deliberately avoiding excitement – but of course does not ask why the Labour Party could not generate enthusiasm.

modest little man with plenty to be modest about", but Attlee provided a rather different epitaph for himself:

> *Few thought he was a starter*
> *There were many who thought themselves smarter*
> *But he ended PM*
> *CH and OM*
> *An Earl and a Knight of the Garter.*

David Lloyd George's daughter, Lady Megan Lloyd George, became the subject of several cartoons when she defected from the Liberals to Labour during the 1955 Election campaign - declaring that she wished "to be true to the radical traditions". Yet the Liberal Party and the use of the Liberal name remained much less prominent than in previous campaigns.

In 1955 **Barbara Castle** was a leading member of the left-wing Bevanite Group within the Labour Party, and a member of Labour's National Executive Committee. She was subsequently a leading minister in Harold Wilson's governments, and, at the age of ninety, was happy to discuss the cartoons of the 1955 General Election for this book.

Barbara Castle has many cartoons on the walls of her house, and had felt their impact in her political career - acknowledging that a powerful cartoon may be welcome when it criticises your opponents, but if critical of your own side can have a lasting effect on your supporters. She deplored the power of the right-wing cartoonists in this General Election, recalling that "in 1955, as in other years, a largely Tory press was always looking for a Labour person to demonise." They may have directed their fire at the whole shadow cabinet, but she regretted one target in particular, recalling that in the 1955 campaign "the savage cartoons of Nye Bevan, that warm hearted inventor of the

National Health Service, were unfair and quite possibly damaging."

Barbara Castle's favourite cartoonist from the 1955 General Election was "Vicky" - Victor Weisz - who at that time was working for the pro-Labour *Daily Mirror*. She recalled that Vicky "had the capacity to capture a complex issue", and that his work placed him among the forefront of British political cartoonists, for his drawings were plain and clear and "speak to you from the page." She particularly admired his *Daily Mirror* cartoon of 11 May 1955, showing pensioners wondering if their standard of living would double in twenty-five years - "a good example of Vicky's ability to make a clear point."

The number of unofficial strikes was said to be a factor that deterred people from supporting the Labour Party in the 1955 Election. However, the Conservative government was reluctant to make this a major factor in its campaign, as successive Ministers of Labour had pursued a deliberate policy of not antagonising the trade unions. Sidney Strube's cartoon for Time and Tide, *published on 28 May 1955 but drawn before the Election, forecasts that there will in fact be a problem.*

Personalities in the 1955 Election campaign

Anthony Eden

Anthony Eden was debonair and well dressed, and even had a hat named after him. He was elected an MP in 1923 at the age of twenty-six, and throughout his career specialised in Foreign Affairs. When Stanley Baldwin became Prime Minister in 1935 he made Eden Foreign Secretary, with the less than exhilarating comment "it looks as if it has to be you."

Eden's career stumbled in 1937, when Baldwin resigned and Neville Chamberlain became Prime Minister. Eden agreed with Chamberlain on all significant aspects of Appeasement, but Chamberlain made interventions on foreign affairs without consulting him, and he resigned in 1938. Eden did not join that tiny group of MPs that supported Churchill's opposition to the policy of Appeasement, for he neither approved of Churchill nor at that time disagreed with Appeasement. He was what contemporaries called a "One Nation Tory", which meant that he did not believe in unnecessarily grinding the faces of the poor.

In 1940 Eden returned for the duration of the war as Churchill's Foreign Secretary. In opposition after 1945, he was again Foreign Secretary under Churchill from 1951. On Churchill's resignation in 1955 he was his obvious and accepted successor, although Eden had a less than satisfactory period as Prime Minister, particularly over the discreditable Suez War. Churchill certainly had major reservations about him, even when allowances are made for the fact that few people recognise in their successors qualities equal to their own. Eden matches exactly Tacitus's comment about the Roman Emperor, Galba, that no one would have doubted his capacity as Emperor if he had never reached that position.

R.A. Butler

R.A. Butler - known as "Rab" - was elected as an MP in 1929, and held a series of junior ministerial posts in the prewar National Governments. Butler attracted attention by his conduct of the government's policy over India, and also as the major spokesman for Appeasement in the House of Commons, whilst the Foreign Secretary, Lord Halifax, sat in the House of Lords. Both roles brought Butler into conflict with Churchill, but to the surprise of many he was retained in Churchill's wartime government, and in 1941 was promoted President of the Board of Education. In this

"WHOEVER COMES BACK WILL HAVE TO DEAL WITH ME!"

capacity Butler introduced 1944 Education Act, providing free secondary education for all.

After the war Butler was a major force in shaping Conservative industrial and economic policy, and after the Conservative Election victory in 1951 he became Chancellor of the Exchequer, which again surprised some. Butler twice acted as Prime Minister during the coinciding illnesses of Churchill and Eden, but then his career took a downward spiral. In 1957, when Eden resigned after Suez, Butler was expected to become Prime Minister, but the Conservative Party - which did not vote directly for its leader in such circumstances - preferred Harold Macmillan. Macmillan's certainty, first for going in and then for coming out of the Suez operation, apparently counted more than Butler's ambiguity about whether or not he was ambivalent.

Under Macmillan Butler served as Home Secretary and deputy Prime Minister, and he reappears in cartoons of the General Elections of 1959 and 1964. Physical changes in his face, not fully represented in the cartoons, gave him an image of flabbiness which in 1963 seemed reflected in his unwillingness to fight over the succession to Macmillan. Butler served as Foreign Secretary to the new Prime Minister, Alec Douglas-Home, until he accepted a peerage in 1965.

The Results of the 1955 General Election

The Conservatives received 49.7% of the votes cast, which was the highest percentage achieved by any party after 1945, and increased their overall majority from 17 to 58. The results were:

Conservatives	344	49.7%
Labour	277	46.4%
Liberal	6	2.7%
Other	2	1.1%
Speaker	1	

Some 76.8% of the electorate voted, which was 5.7% less than 1951 and may reflect the contemporary view that this was a dull Election.

The Cartoonist of the 1955 General Election

Leslie Illingworth has been chosen as the cartoonist of the 1955 Election both for the range and the power of his work. Illingworth started as political cartoonist on the *Western Mail* in Wales in 1921, but from 1927 he had no regular platform for his political work until he joined the *Daily Mail* in 1939. Illingworth worked on that paper for thirty years, and from 1945 was also one of the political cartoonists on *Punch*.

Illingworth's skills as a draughtsman were much admired by his contemporaries. As his work for the 1955 Election demonstrates, his content though not his draughtsmanship differed quite noticeably when drawing for the *Daily Mail* and for *Punch*. The difference was not simply due to the extra space he had in the magazine, for his work on the mass-circulation *Daily Mail* is both more overtly Conservative and more obviously violent than his drawings for Punch.

Illingworth retired from the *Daily Mail* in 1969, but in 1974 he returned to Fleet Street to spend two years as guest cartoonist on the *News of the World*. Unlike his great contemporaries Vicky and Low, there is no major published collection of Illingworth's work.

Chapter 5

"Supermac" Triumphant.

The Run-up to the 1959 General Election

Eden's success in the 1955 Election was quickly followed by criticism - even in Conservative newspapers - of his capacity as a leader. Claims that he could not provide the smack of firm government, plus inaccurate references to his involvement in pre-war Appeasement, may have been factors in his decision to respond strongly to the crisis over the Suez Canal in 1956. The Egyptian leader, Gamal Abdel Nasser, announced that the Canal was to be taken back into Egyptian ownership, and when it became clear that diplomatic efforts by countries including Australia and the United States would have no effect on this decision, Eden decided to use force to "re-open the Canal".

"SHH, SOFTLY, SOFTLY, BOYS—REMEMBER, WE DON'T WANT TO WAKE HIM UP!"

Vicky's cartoon "Shh, Softly, Softly, Boys...", in the Evening Standard *of 14 September 1959, returns to the familiar cartoonist's theme of political apathy. In imitation of the popular Ted Heath Dance Band, Vicky has drawn a band of senior Conservatives led by the Chief Whip, Edward Heath, and featuring Macmillan as a singer dressed in teddy boy clothes. Heath attempts to control Hailsham, Butler, Heathcote Amory (Chancellor of the Exchequer), and Charles Hill, with Lennox Boyd (Secretary for the Colonies) on the double bass. Vicky has a sly extra dig at Selwyn Lloyd (Foreign Secretary), who tinkles a triangle, representing Vicky's view of his lack of significance in the government.*

" I thought your shirt was off-white — until I saw yours ! "

The precise nature of the underlying "collusion" between the British, French and Israeli Governments, which involved the invasion of Egypt, became clear only gradually. The Labour Party and others - including a minority of Conservatives - opposed the intervention even before the details of collusion became known, and their revelation brought further problems. The Chancellor of the Exchequer, Harold Macmillan, was at first a vociferous supporter of intervention, but when he found that the United States was denying Britain the necessary financial support, in anger at Eden's deception, he became a foremost figure in urging its termination.

Eden's physical resilience and nervous system collapsed under the strain. In January 1957 he resigned, and Macmillan, rather than the more ambivalent Butler, emerged from the crisis as the new Conservative Prime Minister. Macmillan projected an image far removed from his supposed plebeian background in the Scottish isles, and was upper class in voice and mannerisms. He generated an air of unflappability, most clearly expressed in 1958 when he referred to the resignation of his Chancellor and two senior Treasury ministers as "a little local difficulty" - the word local serving to remind people that he was off on a Commonwealth Tour.

On the Labour side, Hugh Gaitskell had defeated both Bevan and Morrison to become leader of the Labour Party in December 1955. Bevan gradually accepted this political reality, and in 1957 further dismayed his political supporters by also accepting the need to keep the H-bomb. Bevan wanted to negotiate it away, rather than surrendering it unilaterally, and in a characteristically colourful phrase he denied any virtue in "going naked into the conference chamber". There was party conflict over events in the remaining territories of the British Commonwealth, but this had little

Cummings' cartoon "I thought your shirt was off-white...", in the Daily Express *of 18 September 1959, was another illustration of the mud-slinging theme, this time parodying washing-powder advertisements on the new commercial television. Unusually for Cummings his cartoon does actually identify some disadvantageous features of the Conservative government.*

reverberation with the electorate. An indication of deeper problems to come were the first significant street demonstrations against coloured immigrants.

During the early period of his Prime Ministership, Macmillan managed brilliantly to be both strong in defence of British interests, yet diplomatic in actually pursuing them. He continued the managed dissolution of the British Empire, and presided over a successful economy - albeit with flutters of apprehension about inflation and unemployment. Prosperity - or materialism as some in the Labour Party preferred to call it - was a significant element in contemporary political debate. Rab Butler's comment about rising living standards was put more colloquially by Macmillan, who in July 1957 declared "Let's be frank about it; most of our people have never had it so good". The caveats which followed this assertion were widely ignored - particularly by cartoonists.

On 24 September 1959 Philip Zec - recently moved from the Daily Mirror *to the* Daily Herald *- attacked what he felt were the broken promises of the Conservative Government. Hailsham, Selwyn Lloyd, Butler and Macmillan appear as flies stuck on flypaper - a metaphor that has lost its impact over the years.*

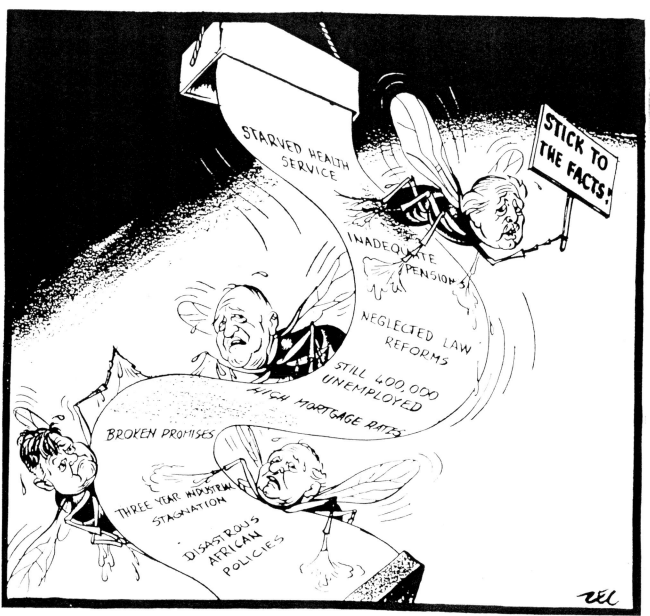

"Stick to them? You're STUCK with 'em!"

In his editorial cartoon for the Sunday Express *of 27 September 1959, Cummings used his familiar "Mr Rising Price" to loom over Gaitskell's promises to the floating voter.*

"WHO , ME ?"

Lord Hailsham's denunciation of mud-slinging was followed by another speech implying that a Labour government would be taken over by militants. His name splits rather neatly to make Vicky's point in "Who...me?" from the Evening Standard *of 28 September 1959.*

Election Issues and the 1959 Election Campaign

On 8 September the Election was announced for 8 October 1959. The Conservatives planned to press home their achievements with the campaign slogan "Life's better under Conservatives. Don't let Labour ruin it" - a less punchy version of Macmillan's "never had it so good" of two years earlier. In contrast Labour hoped to win by attacking complacency, and its manifesto proposed both the abolition of the 11+ examination for secondary school entry, and a full national superannuation scheme with an immediate ten shillings a week pension increase. A scandal in the City also enabled Labour to make vague references to unearned benefits, but on 16 September 1959 Lord Hailsham, the Conservative Party Chairman, repudiated mud slinging between politicians, thus creating a theme on which the cartoonists happily seized. If Hailsham had carried this through it really would have been self-abnegation on a grand scale, but he continued to be as good at slinging mud as anybody else - which was fortunate for the vulgar enjoyment of this and subsequent General Elections.

Both Bevan and Gaitskell were in Moscow at the start of the Election, which enabled them to both start and continue the Election campaign in a new spirit of harmony. On 28 September 1959 Gaitskell declared his commitment to "no increase in standard or other rates of income tax as long as normal peacetime conditions continue". Since Labour's programme implied significant extra expenditure - for example on pensions - he was naturally attacked. It was pointed out that with its planned reduction in purchase tax Labour would not be able to pay for its

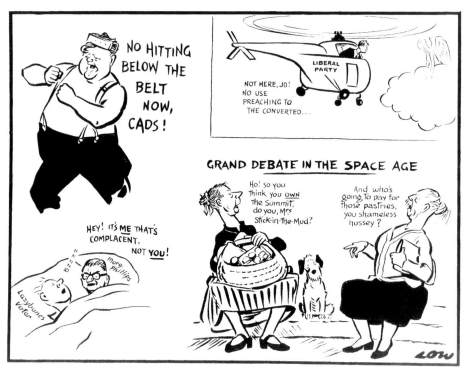

In the Manchester Guardian of 2 October 1959, David Low also made use of Hailsham's supposed high-mindedness in his cartoon "Democracy Rises to its Responsibility". Other panels in this composite cartoon feature Morgan Phillips - the General Secretary of the Labour Party, who had criticised "don't know" voters, Jo Grimond - the Liberal leader who used a helicopter to tour target seats, and Gaitskell and Macmillan as combative housewives.

programme, and Macmillan accused Gaitskell of conducting an auction - in which of course Macmillan with his high moral tone refused to participate.

Current issues about continental Europe were largely ignored during the campaign, as were previous party differences over Kenya, Cyprus and Central Africa. Suez and the Russian-led takeover in Hungary had long passed into memory, and the 1959 Election campaign focused primarily on issues of affluence, and of who would manage it best. These and other issues were now capable of being ventilated on television, as 70% of the electorate owned television sets. Both the BBC and the relatively new independent television companies were prepared to discuss political issues during the Election campaign, and even to allow relatively ordinary electors to debate the issues. Macmillan and Gaitskell did not of course debate directly on television - even in the United States Presidential debates were not televised until 1960 - but their broadcasts were watched by about 20% of the electorate.

Emmwood's cartoon "The Desiccated Calculating Machine", in the Daily Mail of 3 October 1959, refers to Bevan's famous dismissal of Gaitskell. Bevan and Harold Wilson wait for the results, whilst Gaitskell attempts to process the awkward question posed by Harold Macmillan and Iain Macleod.

Cummings' "Election Spotlight", in the Sunday Express *of 4 October 1959, returned to the theme of Gaitskell's promises, with a rather neat representation which at least allowed that Gaitskell might have a conscience. The captions given here were suggested by Cummings on his original drawing.*

" ~~Oh no! Surely! That's not me?~~ "

" Good Heavens, is that really me ? "

Ted Heath recalls the 1959 General Election campaign: "The 1959 General Election was one of the most exciting and difficult in my career. 1955-1959 Parliament had begun for us with the Suez debacle, the resignation of Anthony Eden and his replacement as Prime Minister by Harold Macmillan. Although the popularity of the Government had improved following cuts in income and purchase tax and the duty on beer, it was by no means certain that the Conservative Party would win.

I believe that my contribution to our victory came not so much during the campaign itself, but through my work as Chief Whip in restoring morale within the Party following Suez to the point where our members felt that there was a real chance of winning.

The 1959 General Election also marked a watershed in electioneering: it was the first campaign in which television played a major part. Harold Macmillan disliked the new medium. Ironically, despite calling television studios a 'twentieth century torture chamber' Harold got the best of the television coverage much to Labour's dismay.

They had hoped to use their election broadcasts masterminded by Tony Benn, to present Hugh Gaitskell as the country's next Prime Minister. The Conservatives got back with a majority of one hundred. The Labour Party under Neil Kinnock made the same mistake in 1992 at their triumphalist Sheffield Rally, with the result that Conservatives were again returned to office."

"Floating" voters who have not made up their mind are a major concern for politicians at election time. In "Closing in for the Kill" from the Daily Mail *of 5 October 1959, Leslie Illingworth portrays the "Don't Know" voter stalked by Gaitskell as a tiger, and Jo Grimond, Leader of the Liberal Party, as a forked-tongued serpent. Bevan and Morgan Phillips look ready to attack from their tree, but the lion Macmillan is rather less threatening, whilst the small-scale Wilson smiles benignly.*

Personalities of the 1959 General Election

Harold Macmillan

Before the war Macmillan was a Conservative MP whose left-wing views were unpopular with the Party leadership. In 1938 he had gone so far as to write his own book on politics entitled "The Middle Way", and, since he was also an opponent of Appeasement, he did not gain a government office until 1940, when Churchill became Prime Minister. In 1951 Churchill gave him the task of meeting the Conservative promise to build 300,000 houses in 1951, and his success led to his elevation under Eden first to Foreign Secretary and then to Chancellor.

At the time of the 1959 Election, Macmillan was at the height of his powers. Somehow - like Harold Wilson after him - Macmillan had developed from being a speaker who emptied the House of Commons, to one whose speeches became collector's items full of what parliament generally regards as wit. He had already presented the nation with two soundbites - "never had it so good" and "a little local difficulty" - and in 1960 would make his historic "wind of change" speech. Macmillan also had a reputation for unflappability, although this would be destroyed in 1962 when he sacked a third of his Cabinet - producing one of the best parliamentary jokes from Jeremy Thorpe: "Greater love hath no man than this: that he lay down his friends for his life."

Like much else about him, Macmillan's unflappability was in fact a pose - he was often physically sick before debates. In 1958 the cartoonist Vicky had tried to capture what he saw as Macmillan's essential emptiness in the famous parody of him as "Supermac". To Vicky's dismay, people did not see the intended irony of a figure padded out to look successful, but took it as a genuine compliment. Vicky would probably have done better to continue his portrayal of Macmillan as "the great entertainer".

Hugh Gaitskell

Hugh Gaitskell joined the Labour Party during the General Strike of 1926, but his background as an Oxford-educated economics lecturer always brought resentment from the Left that he had not been born into the Party. Elected to Parliament in 1945, Gaitskell quickly made the first step into government, and in 1950 became a major figure in the Labour Party when Attlee made him Chancellor of the Exchequer.

As with many people of high principle, Gaitskell was unbending once he had decided what that principle was. It was Gaitskell who precipitated the split with Bevan over financial management, and although this did so much to damage the Labour Party it provided good themes for cartoonists.

In December 1955 the Labour MPs - who still elected the Party leader - chose Gaitskell in preference to either the disturbing Bevan or the ageing Morrison. Bevan remarked that "The right kind of leader for the Labour Party is a desiccated calculating machine", and although he denied that this was meant to apply to Gaitskell his denial is rather unconvincing, since there were no other desiccated calculating machines in sight.

By 1959, Gaitskell had a reputation as a sound but unexciting leader, who believed in rationality and tried to encourage equality of opportunity. After 1959 the picture was modified, and in 1960 his famous speech against unilateral nuclear disarmament was unequalled in its impact in any Party Conference. However, Gaitskell proved unable to tackle successfully the issue of Clause Four in the Labour Party's Constitution. This committed the party to common ownership of the means of production, distribution and exchange, and although no longer a serious political policy it represented something important to both Labour militants and Conservative opponents.

THE RE-THINKER

Low's cartoon "The Re-Thinker", from the Manchester Guardian *of 13 October 1959, post-dates the election but is a fascinating image that resonates today. In a parody of Rodin's sculpture "The Thinker", Gaitskell considers the future of his party. After the defeat of 1959 he made a failed attempt to remove the commitment to nationalisation enshrined in Clause Four of its constitution, but this was not actually done until Tony Blair took charge of the Labour Party nearly forty years later.*

The Results of the 1959 General Election

There was never any considerable danger that the Conservatives would lose the 1959 General Election despite Gaitskell's very real beliefs to the contrary. The turnout - 78.7% - was larger than in the 1955 General Election, but both the Conservative and Labour Parties gained less of the vote because the Liberals more than doubled their share - although still securing only a small number of seats.

Conservatives	365	49.4%
Labour	258	43.8%
Liberals	6	5.9%
Others	1	1.0%

The Cartoonist of the 1959 General Election

"Vicky" - Victor Weisz - has been selected as cartoonist of the 1959 Election, not for a single cartoon but for several. Vicky was born in Berlin of Hungarian Jewish parents, and after early non-political work in Germany he arrived in London in 1935. Vicky worked for a number of newspapers and magazines before joining the staff of the *News Chronicle* - a Liberal paper - as political cartoonist in 1939.

At the *News Chronicle* Vicky was famously advised by the editor to steep himself in British culture if he was to be a successful political cartoonist. The expression of this is to be found in many of his cartoons, which have references to things an educated British public was expected to be interested in, and knowledgeable about - such as Shakespeare and Dickens. Among cartoonists of today only Nicholas Garland includes such references in his work.

Some of Vicky's cartoons were rejected by the *News Chronicle*, but he subsequently and uniquely had them published as "The Editor Regrets". In 1954 Vicky left the *News Chronicle* for the pro-Labour *Daily Mirror*, but in 1958 he transferred to the *Evening Standard* and almost immediately launched his "Supermac" character. A devout Socialist, it seems from letters to the editor that many of the *Evening Standard*'s readers disliked Vicky. Lt Col G.L. Thompson called one of his cartoons "a masterpiece of Socialist propaganda, vulgar, vindictive and misleading", although another reader described the cartoonist himself as "clever and very tolerant, which is more than can be said of his detractors."

The examples shown here illustrate that Vicky had a greater range than was often presumed. Like many cartoonists he was better at capturing some politicians than others. His portrayal of Macmillan as "Supermac" famously rebounded when many readers did not recognise the irony, but Leslie Illingworth believed that Vicky was responsible for destroying Sir Alec Douglas Home at the 1964 General Election by portraying him as weak and silly.

Vicky's commitment to politics reached an unfortunate and final expression in 1966, when he committed suicide during a bout of depression supposedly induced by his views on Harold Wilson's Labour Government. Vicky was often criticised for the "viciousness" of his cartoons, but by comparison with modern cartoonists also accused of "savagery" he can be seen to have more frequently used satire, irony and the juxtaposition of opposites to achieve his ends.

Chapter 6

White Heat or Matchsticks?

Stanley Franklin's cartoon "The Wilsun", in the Daily Mirror *of 14 September 1964, shows Home trying unavailingly to extinguish the Labour manifesto with a hosepipe, while Hogg is shown ringing the bell which helped establish his political fame many years earlier. Franklin was drawing for the only newspaper committed to the Labour cause.*

The Wilsun

The Run-up to the 1964 General Election

The period between 1959 and 1964 was a time of gradually declining popularity for the Tories. At first the Liberals picked up the disaffected vote, but from 1962 the Labour Party experienced an increase in popularity. In July 1962 Macmillan's vaunted unflappability as Prime Minister was permanently destroyed when he sacked a third of his Cabinet, following bad by-election results.

In 1962 the Conservative government's management of the economy also switched from restraint under Selwyn Lloyd as Chancellor, to expansion under his successor, Reginald Maudling. Lloyd's attempts to influence the economy through a tripartite National Economic Development

Bill Papas, in his cartoon for the
Guardian *of 15 September 1964,*
has Wilson and Home
hammering the floating voter,
while Jo Grimond, the Leader of
the Liberal Party, takes a
different stance. The Guardian
was naturally sympathetic to the
Liberal Party, but wanted a
Labour government.

Psssst!

Council, a National Incomes Commission, and a Pay Pause had been
difficult for Labour to criticise, but had produced no particular credit for
him or the government. Macmillan's pre-war memories of unemployment
in Stockton on Tees were always said to influence his attitude to financial
management, and presumably influenced his choice of Maudling as
Chancellor.

As Prime Minister, Macmillan seemed happier on the international stage.
In 1960 he scored a notable success with his "Wind of Change" speech in
South Africa, signalling the end of Empire, and he was the first British
Prime Minister to make a clear decision to join the European Economic

Illingworth's cartoon in the
Daily Mail *of 25 September*
1964 draws a comparison
between the supposed
modernisation of the Labour
Party, in a smart new car,
and what he saw as the

Cummings

"Good Heavens! Our Doomsday Weapon has broken loose!"

Hogg Bomb

ALARM

Community. This gave Ted Heath his first major experience of international negotiation, but not everyone was pleased to see the end of an attitude represented by the famous headline "Continent cut off by fog", and in 1963 President De Gaulle of France vetoed British entry.

As Leader of the Opposition, Hugh Gaitskell continued to show that Bevan had been wrong to call him a "desiccated calculating machine". In an impassioned oration at the Labour Party Conference in 1960 Gaitskell rejected unilateral nuclear disarmament and promised to "fight, fight and fight again for the Labour Party we love". His subsequent decision to oppose entry to Europe, and his reference to its threatening "one thousand years of history", were greeted with rather less acclaim by many of his supporters, but the success of such speeches helped him to establish his position as a strong and effective leader.

By the end of 1962 memories of Gaitskell's ineffective attempt to change "Clause Four" of the Labour Party Constitution appeared much less important. However, at the beginning of 1963 Gaitskell died suddenly aged

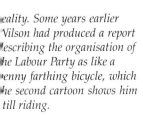

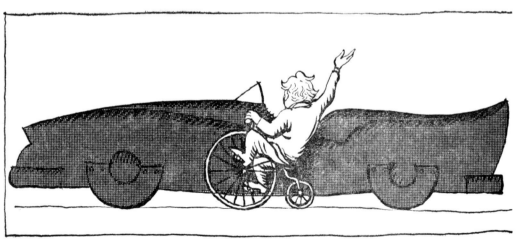

As with his predecessor David Low, Vicky's cartoons in the Evening Standard *often produced unfavourable comments from Conservative readers. His cartoon of 28 September 1964 shows typical Tory readers delighted to find not only Vicky in the stocks, but the BBC also declaring a moratorium on political satire.*

"Ah, jolly funny! At last a decent, unbiased, non-political election cartoon—just like the good old BBC!"

only fifty-six. In the subsequent leadership election George Brown, a right winger who could be as intemperate - in both senses of the word - as Nye Bevan, was defeated by Harold Wilson, who had acquired a left wing reputation in 1951 by leaving the Attlee Government with Nye Bevan.

Macmillan proved reluctant to leave the political stage, despite evidence of his growing unpopularity. There was a general feeling that he had lost his hold over the audience, and he was seen as out of touch for believing that his War Minister, John Profumo, had not lied to the House of Commons. Macmillan's illness was also a continuing problem, and in October 1963 he decided that the show could no longer go on. His resignation turned out to be unnecessary in health terms, but it did not damage Tory prospects.

Macmillan was succeeded by Sir Alec Douglas Home, who emerged - through a partly mystical process - as having either more support, or less opposition, than Rab Butler. The supposedly devious Butler had "made no arrangements", and was surprised as Home backed into the limelight. The fact the Conservatives had initially been so undecided between four candidates, and had then finished up with a largely unknown leader, did nothing to add to the credibility of the Conservative government.

In order to sit in the House of Commons, and become a leadership candidate, Home had surrendered his title, the 14th Earl of Home, as had Viscount Hailsham, who reverted to being Quintin Hogg. The procedure for surrendering titles had been fought for by the Labour MP Anthony Wedgwood Benn, formerly Viscount Stansgate – not

Vicky in the Evening Standard *of 29 September 1964 refers to Home's gaffe in calling the supplementary pension a "donation" to pensioners. As the Labour government was to discover thirty-five years later, insults to pensioners were regarded with particular disfavour.*

"SIR ALEC SAYS HE'LL GIVE US A DONATION WHEN WE'RE A BIT OLDER . . ."

"I wish to heaven I could be a one-man-band!"

During the 1964 General Election campaign Wilson was accused of running a one-man band, but in the Daily Express of 30 September 1964 Cummings showed him being hit by George Brown's blast about a supposed three percent mortgage, despite his encouraging the Labour orchestra to play pianissimo.

the last time in which the future Tony Benn would prove of assistance to the Conservative Party. However, Harold Wilson's attempt to capitalise on the fact that he was the "Fourteenth Earl", was disarmed by an unusual shaft of wit when Home referred to him as the "Fourteenth Mr Wilson".

Election Issues and the 1964 Campaign

Wilson had the advantage of being much better known than Home, and had also been leader of his party for twenty-one months before Home became Prime Minister. Yet Home showed Prime Ministerial grit by making the decision to hold the Election as late as possible, and it was announced on 15 September for 15 October 1964.

Wilson had already set Labour's agenda, especially in his conference speech of 1963, in which he talked about "the white heat of the new industrial revolution". Labour's Election campaign hammered at the low growth rate in the economy, and at what they described as the Tories' stop-go economic policies. Their manifesto focused on the need for growth through innovation and efficiency, and proposed a major national planning initiative, to be conducted through a new Ministry of Economic Affairs. Home delivered a stinging blow by describing the Labour manifesto as "a menu without Prices" - a theme to which the Conservatives returned throughout the Election.

Not surprisingly - since Home was much more comfortable with foreign affairs - the Conservatives emphasised their policy on defence, and in particular Britain's retention of its nuclear deterrent. Pensions were also an issue of the campaign, and, much less happily for Home, he referred to a supplementary pension as "a donation" during one of the new relatively-testing television interviews. This was remembered, while Wilson's one explicit gaffe, when he attempted to blame Tory shop stewards for strikes, got lost rather quickly. Labour still retained proposals for the

'In the name of political balance, isn't it time Hogg said something?'

nationalisation of steel and water, but managed to avoid any serious discussion of issues around trade unions and restrictive practices.

Two major figures who were expected to commit errors did relatively well. George Brown, Labour's deputy leader, had only one lapse when he referred to the possibility of cutting mortgages to three percent - which may not have been disadvantageous to Labour. For the Conservatives, Quintin Hogg tried to defend the government over the Profumo affair by implying there were adulterers on the Labour Front Bench. However accurate this may have been, it was viewed with some distaste, and gave Hogg the distinction of receiving the last electoral rebuke from Earl Attlee. (Churchill, only a few months away from death, did not speak during the Election.)

In the New Statesman *of 2 October 1964, "Trog" - Wally Fawkes - returns to the mutual fears of Wilson and Home. George Brown is shown campaigning with a three percent mortgage in his pocket, while Wilson asks for a similar indiscretion from the Tories.*

Immigration, which had been raised for the first time in 1959, did not become a full national issue in the 1964 Election campaign, but it did emerge in relation to one particular constituency - Smethwick - where Wilson tried unavailingly to press Home to withdraw his support from a supposedly racist Tory candidate. Labour had opposed the Commonwealth Immigration Act of 1962, but no political capital was made from this in the national campaign on either side.

Television coverage of the Election included even more free debate than before, but the leaders did not

John Jensen's cartoon in the Sunday Telegraph *of 4 October 1964 quotes an earlier pious statement by Harold Wilson, whilst suggesting that he has in fact engaged in personal attacks and misrepresentations during the Election campaign.*

face each other directly. The Conservatives tried to portray themselves as a team, not a one-man band, but the campaign was undoubtedly dominated by Wilson at the expense of Home. Except for some successful heckling of Hogg and Home, and some unsuccessful heckling of Wilson - who played it rather well - the 1964 Election campaign was in fact regarded as unexpectedly dull.

Denis Healey remembers the 1964 Election: "Labour fought the 1964 election with every confidence of victory; but so we had in 1959. So I was immensely relieved when the first results showed an undeniable swing to Labour. It was an extraordinary day. I was touring the polling stations in East Leeds when I heard that Krushchev had been removed from power in Moscow. Robin Day interviewed me in Leeds Town Hall at one in the morning, after my re-election had been announced; he was more interested in Krushchev's fall than in my own good fortune or the Labour Party's return to power.

I went to bed at three o'clock. It then looked as if Labour would have an overall majority of about twenty seats. But when, after a few hours sleep, Edna and I started the long drive back to London, we heard on the car radio our majority melting away, as the results came in from scattered rural constituencies. By the time we reached our home in Highgate, Labour's overall majority had shrunk to four. And China had just exploded its first atom bomb – using, as I heard later, a technique which none of the existing nuclear powers had adopted.

I scarcely had time to unpack before Harold Wilson called me to No. 10 Downing Street and offered me the Ministry of Defence, saying he had already told the Queen of my acceptance. There followed a weekend of pandemonium, in which only my excitement at my new job kept my post-election exhaustion at bay."

Cartoonists like to establish reference to contemporaneous issues - in this case the 1964 Tokio Olympics, which began during the General Election campaign. Vicky's cartoon "We Stand on Our Record!", in the Evening Standard *of 7 October 1964, shows the major figures in Home's Cabinet as athletes resting on their failures. On the far left is Henry Brooke - the Home Secretary, with Heath, Selwyn Lloyd, Home, Butler, Maudling and Hogg.*

"WE STAND ON OUR RECORD!"

AND
CUMMINGS'
VIEWPOINT..:

"Scaremonger! I've been conferring with my matches and all is well!"

THE
BALANCE
OF
PAYMENTS

Cummings

In the Daily Express of 7 October 1964, Cummings' "Scaremonger!" cartoon was more critical of the Conservative government than usual. The balance of payments figures which came out late in the Election were disadvantageous to the government - as was Home's earlier admission that he had to use a box of matches to understand economics.

*As if responding to Jensen's
attack on Wilson in the*
Sunday Telegraph, *Vicky's
cartoon "Who? Me?", in the*
Evening Standard *of 8
October 1964, resurrected
Quintin Hogg's pious
statement about mud-slinging
which he made five years
earlier.*

"WHO? ME?"

Personalities of the 1964 General Election Campaign

Alec Douglas Home

Alec Douglas Home initially acquired fame as a Conservative MP in 1938, when he was photographed carrying Chamberlain's bags on his return from the final attempt to appease Hitler at Munich. Home returned to parliament in 1950, and in 1951 - after becoming 14th Earl of Home - he became a Minister for Scotland. This was Home's only experience of a significant domestic ministerial post, since he was subsequently Commonwealth Secretary and then Foreign Secretary.

Whether this latter appointment was a major compliment to Home's ability, or to Macmillan's disdain for opponents of the House of Lords, was never clear. In 1963 Macmillan favoured Home as his successor, rather than his initial choice of Quintin Hogg, partly because of Home's inability to make either enemies or memorable remarks. However, when Home became Prime Minister there were senior cabinet members who clearly thought him a bad choice, and Macleod and Powell from the previous cabinet refused to serve under him.

Home's strength was in foreign affairs, and his gentlemanly manner and apparent lack of naked ambition did not serve well against Harold Wilson. Home made the unfortunate admission that when considering economic documents he would take out a box of matches and start moving them around. This was thought to illustrate his poor grasp of economics - particularly in comparison to Wilson - and was seized on by cartoonists. Home was also visually unprepossessing, another point on which cartoonists were particularly cruel. In his autobiography he reported disarmingly that one make-up artist abandoned her attempt to make him look any better, because she said he had a head like a skull. Home joked to the audience at one of his meetings that "I am not a bit like you see me on television", but the problem was that most people only saw him on television.

Home's lasting contribution to the Conservative Party may well have been to ensure that its future leaders were elected rather than "emerging". He conducted himself with grace and loyalty in relation to his successor, Ted Heath, under whom he served as Foreign Secretary.

Mens sana in corpore sano ?

Bill Papas' cartoon "Mens Sana In Corpore Sano", in the Guardian *of 14 October 1964, shows the average voters examining the major candidates. A corpulent Hogg stands next to a very thin Home, followed by Butler, Selwyn Lloyd and Maudling. Wilson alone represents the Labour Party, with Grimond, Leader of the Liberal Party, shown as a fine upstanding fellow. Readers of the* Guardian *were expected to know that the Latin title meant "a healthy mind in a healthy body".*

Quintin Hogg

Quintin Hogg first successfully stood as an MP at a famous by-election in Oxford in 1938. Here he supported Appeasement, which seems peculiarly uncharacteristic given his later bellicosity in public speeches. Hogg was a very effective conference performer, and cartoonists had great fun when as Party Chairman he rang a hand bell at a Conservative Conference. In fact they continued to have fun with him through his political career, until he landed on the Woolsack as Lord Chancellor in Thatcher's Government.

Hogg had a reputation as an extremely clever man, which did not seem to match his choleric outbursts on television and on Election hustings. In 1963, for reasons which have never been clear, Macmillan initially chose Hogg to succeed him as Prime Minister, and Hogg renounced his hereditary title. However, Hogg's enthusiasm about his own candidature, plus the general air of excitability he created, and a rousing but indelicate personal offer of his candidature around the coincidental Tory Party Conference, caused Macmillan to withdraw his support.

For years a cartoonist's delight, Hogg's misfortune was that his name varied between being Quintin Hogg and Viscount Hailsham, although the constant attraction for cartoonists was not who he was but what he said.

Harold Wilson

Harold Wilson was a Yorkshire-born economist of some brilliance, who in 1947 went from being a very effective civil servant to early success in Attlee's government as President of the Board of Trade. Wilson changed his physical appearance by shaving off his moustache, but the changes in his personality and beliefs were more difficult to identify.

Initially a dull speaker who could empty the House of Commons, Wilson later became famous for his wit. In 1951 his resignation with Nye Bevan was a surprise, but it gave him a reputation as a left winger which lasted until he became Prime Minister in 1964. In fact Wilson quickly abandoned the pure milk of Bevanism, and became his own man, whatever that was. Gaitskell was appropriately suspicious of him, though he gave him major responsibilities in shadowing the Exchequer and Foreign Affairs.

After the death of Gaitskell in 1964, Wilson defeated both George Brown and Jim Callaghan for the leadership of the Labour Party. By the time of the General Election he had established himself as a commanding figure, not least because he lived by his own belief that politics was a matter of pragmatism rather than ideology. Wilson's main history is after the 1964 Election, when what had been regarded as sensible flexibility came to be seen in less glowing terms: as one of his colleagues put it, if he was to eat a nail it would turn into a screw.

Wilson's disdain for strategy was shown in his comment that "A week in politics is a long time", but he nevertheless won two elections, retired at a time of his own choosing, and kept the Labour Party together - a feat which caused admiration and regret in different people. Ian Macleod - one of his Tory opponents - captured Wilson brilliantly. Noting that John F. Kennedy described himself as "an idealist without illusion", Macleod called Wilson "an illusionist without ideals."

George Brown

George Brown was a genuinely working-class Labour politician, who entered parliament in 1945 after a period as a Trades Union leader. Brown was self-educated, having left school at fifteen, but he was always respected by his civil servants as having a first-class - though untrained - mind. In 1951 Attlee gave Brown a middle-level government role as Minister of Works, and in 1960 he was elected deputy leader of the Labour Party in preference to Harold Wilson.

Brown attracted admiration and affection from some colleagues, but others regarded his volcanic temperament - with its occasional outbursts of highly-coloured language - as wholly disabling him for the office of party leader, let alone Prime Minister. Whereas Quintin Hogg's outbursts were thought to be part of his nature, in Brown's case they were often precipitated by over-indulgence in alcohol, and although he may have added greatly to the gaiety and attraction of politics, he did himself no favours in public perception by allowing this indulgence to outweigh his serious side.

Unlike other cartoonists, Illingworth was prepared to draw Home as a relatively distinguished figure - as in his cartoon "The winning card?" from the Daily Mail *of 14 October 1964. The "Time for a Change" card was not in fact played very strongly during the General Election, although the "Prosperity" card was - unsuccessfully as it turned out.*

In 1963 Brown was defeated by Wilson in the leadership contest, and, after a few days depression, decided to accommodate himself to a leader for whom he had no personal respect. After the 1964 Election Brown was an extraordinarily energetic producer of ideas for the new National Plan, which sadly foundered under the impact of economic reality. In 1966 he became an equally energetic Foreign Secretary, until he eventually decided that he had had enough of what he saw as Wilson's inappropriate style of government, and resigned in 1968.

The Results of the 1964 General Election

The turnout in the 1964 General Election was slightly down at 77.1%. The final Labour majority was only four, although the Conservatives lost sixty seats. There has been some dispute among historians as to whether Home's relative unattractiveness contributed to the Tory's defeat; but it would be even more difficult to assess whether Gaitskell could have secured a larger majority for Labour. The Liberals gained their highest percentage of the poll since 1929.

Labour	317	44.1%
Conservatives	304	43.4%
Liberal	9	11.2%
Other	0	1.3%

The Cartoonist of the 1964 General Election

Bill Papas was one of the many foreign-born cartoonists to work successfully in the United Kingdom. Of Greek origin, he was born in South Africa and started his political cartoon work on the *Cape Times*. Papas transferred to London in 1959, and did work for *Punch* and the *Sunday Times* before joining the *Guardian* in 1963, as its political cartoonist in succession to David Low.

The 1964 General Election was the first that Papas had covered, and his Election cartoons are interesting because they produce a smile rather than a wince - he once said "I don't see the point of dwelling on deformities to bring over the point." Compared with Low, Illingworth and Vicky, his drawings have a rather wispy line, but when necessary they could punch home.

After 1964 Papas shared Vicky's disillusionment with the Labour Government, but showed it in a less extreme form by leaving the United Kingdom in 1969, initially to travel around Greece but then to live permanently in the United States.

Chapter 7

"Labour Government Works."

John Jensen's cartoon "Strange Wooing", in the Sunday Telegraph of 6 March 1966, focuses on the attempts by both Wilson and Heath to attract voters from the middle ground. At the Election the Liberal vote indeed fell by 2.5% and was analysed as having added two votes to Labour for every one to the Conservatives.

The Run-up to the 1966 General Election

Labour won the 1964 General Election, but was obliged to work with a parliamentary majority that never rose above five seats, and could sink as low as one. Yet Harold Wilson still behaved as if he had working majority, and did not attempt a formal pact with the small Liberal Party. Even his Conservative opponents regarded the Prime Minister as a master of tactics - he behaved as if he was leading a tough and competent government, and after the first twelve months the electorate began to believe it.

Labour arrived in office facing a balance of payments crisis, the result of the last Conservative Chancellor's attempt to create growth, and of Labour's own comments about it. An early decision not to devalue the pound - and not to allow any discussion of the decision - became an issue for debate amongst economists but not between the parties. There was some excitement over the problems of steel nationalisation, but Wilson managed to avoid a threatened defeat in the Commons. Labour's attractive proposals on housing and pensions were not implemented during this parliament, but they may well have helped Labour's standing in the opinion polls.

Wilson's decision to put George Brown in charge of a new Department of Economic Affairs was intended both to encourage creative tension between the DEA and the Treasury, and to satisfy Brown's personal ambitions. The DEA was part of Labour's attempt to stimulate greater optimism, but financial problems meant that it was only successful in its efforts to control prices and incomes. It was given no teeth, and although the National Plan may have envisaged an average 3.8% growth rate for the economy, there was no mechanism to achieve that.

In foreign policy, Wilson supported American action in Vietnam, although without sending troops as Attlee had done in Korea. The illegal declaration

The Election debate over the power of trade unions is demonstrated by three cartoons. "If you can't beat 'em - join 'em" by "Eccles" - Frank Brown - in the Communist Daily Worker of 8 March 1966, shows Wilson and George Brown marching alongside Heath in opposition to union power. "Now we Conservatives have the chance..." by George Gale in the left wing Tribune on 18 March 1966, contrasts Edward Heath's tough stance on the unions, with his soft approach to Ian Smith, who had declared independence in Rhodesia in 1965. Illingworth's cartoon for the Daily Mail of 11 March 1966 depicts the trades' union dragon - which Illingworth used frequently in his cartoons - squashing George Brown and his prices and incomes policy, to the dismay of Wilson and his Chancellor, James Callaghan.

If you can't beat 'em — join 'em

"Now we Conservatives have the chance to put forward our own positive policies" Edward Heath

of independence by white Rhodesia also created a major issue for the government, but the Tory front bench supported Wilson's policy of sanctions. In July 1965 Sir Alec Douglas Home resigned as Tory leader, having initiated the process by which the future leader would be elected by MPs, subject to confirmation by a wider Tory electorate. In the resulting contest Edward Heath beat Reginald Maudling and Enoch Powell, his apparent vigour being contrasted with Maudling's more laid-back style.

Election Issues and the 1966 Campaign

The General Election was set for 31 March 1966. Labour ran a generally subdued campaign, and the Conservative attempt to project future triumphs and distance themselves from past failures could not shake up a low-key campaign. Wilson presented the Labour government as efficient, and the slogan offered to the electorate was "You <u>know</u> Labour Government works". The Conservatives sought to present Heath as a more

NO SURPRISES...

...NO LAST MINUTE SECOND THOUGHTS...

...NO REVERSALS OF POLICY...

...NO THEORY...

...NO SOFT EASY PROMISES...

...JUST HARD HEADED REALISM!

Nicholas Garland in the Daily Telegraph *of 9 March 1966 pictured what was already recognised as part of the Wilson persona. The final transformation of Wilson into a fairy turns it from a relatively straightforward cartoon into something more memorable.*

dynamic figure than his leadership rivals, and this was further projected in their Election slogan "Action not Words".

The presentation of Heath as a dynamic new leader was not an impossible task – after all, Wilson had managed it only two years earlier. The Conservative Party had also produced some new policies, especially on Europe, Trade Union Reform and Social Welfare. Yet by March 1966 these new Conservative policies had not become sufficiently grounded to compete successfully with the Labour retort of "Thirteen wasted years". In addition, Heath's relative stiffness contrasted unfavourably with Wilson's slick management of his public image. Heath was not as comfortable on the platform or in the television studios as Wilson, who managed to present himself as Prime Ministerial in his speeches and quick-witted in his response to hecklers.

During the Election campaign Heath made a good joke about Wilson's attention to image, referring to the fact that a giant panda had been sent to Moscow for mating: "In a month's time we will be reading that Mr Wilson is having tea at No. 10 with a pregnant panda." The panda reference appeared in several cartoons, but Wilson came back with an even stronger image relating to the campaign for entry into the Common Market. Heath had been the Minister responsible for the previous attempt to negotiate Britain's entry, and the Conservatives still seemed generally more keen. Wilson described Heath as "Rolling on his back like a spaniel at any kind

Papas in the Guardian *of 9 March 1966 shows Wilson sauntering away from the ruins of his "Socialist Principles", which he has apparently blown up himself. Although Papas does not specify what these were, he identifies an issue on which left wingers already felt let down by Wilson.*

gesture from the French". This possibly had greater impact than Heath's joke over the panda, and Cummings drew a very explicit cartoon of it for the *Daily Express*.

Such excitement as there was emerged from relatively trivial issues on the fringes of the Election campaign. Quintin Hogg did not drop any verbal clangers, but cartoonists seized on an incident in the campaign when he was caught waving his stick during a public meeting. Of greater significance to Labour was the report of a kangaroo court held for trade union members who had not joined an unofficial strike. A "noose" had supposedly been set up as part of the trial, and this was given general attention in the press and by cartoonists, along with other attempts by local trade unions to "discipline" their members.

Despite the fuss over the steel industry, the general question of nationalisation did not become a major element in the campaign, nor did nuclear weapons or the situation in Rhodesia. Heath's attempt to get a serious discussion on inflation in wages and prices - compared with only a one percent increase in production - also made no headway. Heath indeed came over as rather stiff and even shy; and he proved no more of a match for Wilson than Home had been in 1964. Wilson's tactical skills were more evident in the 1966 Election campaign than the mixture of paranoia and Walter Mitty optimism that would characterise his second premiership.

In his Observer *cartoon of 20 March 1966 "Trog" - Wally Fawkes - captures an important aspect of the relationship between political candidates and coloured voters. However, immigration was less of an issue in this campaign by comparison with the 1964 Election, and with what would develop by 1970.*

Now, ideally, we'd like you to vote for our party and not tell anybody.

"Ouch! It's those *ghastly* comprehensive rotters again"

Nicholas Garland's cartoon "Ouch!" in the Daily Telegraph *of 16 March 1966 focuses on a relatively neglected aspect of the Election. Tony Crosland, Secretary of State for Education, had proclaimed that he would destroy every grammar school in pursuit of the Labour policy of setting up comprehensives. Wilson, Crosland and George Brown are shown as schoolboys attacking the shadow Education Secretary, Edward Boyle (dressed as Billy Bunter), Hogg (in an Eton jacket) and Heath (in a uniform perhaps representing his grammar school background).*

Roy Jenkins who had become Home Secretary in December 1965, recalls of the 1966 General Election: "I played an intermediate role in the campaign, a sort of apprentice star, but definitely not a fully fledged one. I had a lucky start to the campaign, with exactly the sort of issue on which I had said I was going to put a new imprint on the Home Office breaking favourably on 4 March 1966. A Surrey child had been instructed by its over-hygienic mother to wipe its cutlery at school. This was against some school regulations, from which stemmed a ridiculous escalation culminating in the child being taking way from the mother and placed in care. Vast publicity was building up. The Prime Minister with his night editor's eye exceptionally telephoned to enquire what we were doing, by which time we were able to tell him that we had settled the matter.

By summoning the Attorney-General, bullying the Home Office, slightly straining the law and speaking faithfully down the telephone to the chairman of the local children's committee, I got the child out of care and back to its mother within a few hours. This was obviously common sense and both press and public (as far as I could tell) applauded. It gave me a favourable wind for the whole campaign, the outcome of which was a Labour majority of ninety-seven and a more favourable swing in Stechford (8.9 per cent) than in any other constituency in Britain."

"Ha, Mr. Heath! You're Just De Gaulle's spaniel!"

In "Ha, Mr. Heath!" - his 21 March 1966 cartoon in the Daily Express - *Cummings picks up Wilson's comment about Heath "rolling on his back like a spaniel" to please de Gaulle, but also adds an image of Wilson being held up by President Lyndon Johnson. The reference was both to Wilson's support of Johnson over Vietnam, and to the less well-known fact that Johnson had upset American animal lovers by holding up a dog.*

"Trouble about you, Heath, is you don't look sincere..."

Cummings' cartoon "Trouble about you, Heath...", in the Daily Express *of 21 March 1966, shows a real Ted Heath confronted by a mechanical Wilson, whose voice comes from records labelled "Honestly", "Frankly" and "Sincerely". Other broken records are labelled with Labour's promises on production, tax and living costs, in imagery that harks back to the portrayal of Wilson's predecessor, Hugh Gaitskell, as a desiccated calculating machine.*

Personality of the 1966 General Election

Edward Heath

In 1965 Edward Heath became the youngest leader the Tories had elected in the twentieth century. He had first entered parliament in 1950, and initially progressed through the Whips Office, an institution whose traditional silence and reticence was thought to explain his later ineffectiveness as a speaker. His interest in the benefits of European co-operation was first demonstrated in 1961, when Macmillan gave him the job of negotiating Britain's entry into the Common Market. Heath had been frustrated by de Gaulle's veto, but at the Board of Trade in 1963 he successfully pushed through the abolition of Retail Price Maintenance, which was seen as a significant change in the British economy.

Elected by his fellow Conservative MPs to confront Harold Wilson, Heath proved unable to do this effectively, either in parliament or in the wider context of the 1966 Election campaign. During this campaign he came across as unrelaxed and humourless, and cartoonists seized on two features closely related to this public perception. They emphasised his fixed smile and particularly his teeth - which gleamed more than any politician until Tony Blair - and they also picked out the way he shook his shoulders very visibly when he wanted to show how amused he was. Heath had many interests apart from politics - in Denis Healey's terms, he had considerable "hinterland". However, his love of music and sailing also became targets for cartoonists.

Heath's loss of the 1966 General Election was unsurprising, but his victory in 1970 was certainly unexpected. However, two General Election defeats in 1974 led to his being replaced the following year by Margaret Thatcher. This ended his front bench career, since she did not follow precedent in offering him a government post in 1979. The discomfort behind this snub was evident at the time, but was later emphasised by Heath's disagreement with many of Mrs Thatcher's policies. In his later years Heath developed a much more relaxed speaking style and occasional wit, and is likely to be complimented by most historians - if not Conservative voters - for sacking Enoch Powell in 1968 and for taking Britain into the EEC.

The Result of the 1966 General Election

At 75.8% of the electorate, the turn out in the 1966 General Election was the lowest since the war. Enthusiasm was particularly low in safe seats, but the voters nevertheless gave Labour a commanding lead at the polls and a significant parliamentary majority:

Labour	363	47.9%
Conservative	253	41.9%
Liberals	12	8.5%
Speaker	1	-
Republican	1	-

The Cartoonist of the 1966 General Election

Norman Mansbridge was a commercial artist who first showed his power as a cartoonist in his illustrations to the 1939 book *Adolf in Blunderland*. Mansbridge contributed to a number of newspapers and magazines, but became closely associated with *Punch*, which first published his work in 1937, and where from 1949 to 1968 he shared with Illingworth the role of political cartoonist.

Mansbridge is a slightly unlikely choice as political cartoonist of the 1966 Election, but has particularly been chosen for his cartoon "Compulsory Education", in *Punch* of 23 March 1966. Here Mansbridge shows Heath and Wilson as teachers dragging the trade unions into school - Heath armed with a cane and Wilson with a book of child psychology. It was unusual for a cartoonist to show the trade unions in such a childlike form, but Mansbridge's schoolboy is certainly not docile, and looks a very traditional representation of a bully. This was certainly a view held of the trade unions by many voters in 1966.

Mansbridge abandoned political cartoons after 1968, in favour of other forms of illustration, including strips for children's comics.

"STEADY HAROLD—IT'S NOT THAT BIG A MAJORITY!"

Labour's success in the 1966 Election was recorded by "Jak" - Raymond Jackson - in his cartoon "Steady Harold" for the Evening Standard *of 1 April 1966. Wilson adopts the familiar posture of President De Gaulle of France, whilst George Brown holds his discarded Gannex raincoat – a favourite "identifier" for cartoonists.*

COMPULSORY EDUCATION

Chapter 8

Wilson Complacent, Heath Persistent.

IF YOU WIN THREE IN A ROW, DOES THAT MAKE IT YOURS OUTRIGHT?

"If you win three in a row..." by "Trog" - Wally Fawkes - in the Daily Mail *of 20 May 1970, is interesting as the first to show a Prime Minister's wife. Wilson was accompanied throughout the Election campaign by his wife Mary, reinforcing his cosy image as a family man in contrast to Heath the bachelor. Trog unfairly makes Mary Wilson seem simple minded, but the cartoon accurately conveys Wilson's feet-up complacency.*

Bill Papas in Punch *of 20 May 1970 expresses what many felt was Wilson's ambiguous position as Labour leader. Hanging on to the coat tails of Conservatism, he is embarrassed to find Socialism still tagging along behind.*

The Run-up to the 1970 General Election

A major economic crisis, the first of several, hit the Labour government almost immediately on its return to power in March 1966. The Cabinet chose deflation rather than devaluation, a policy backed by the Chancellor, Jim Callaghan, and approved without significant debate. Four months after the Election the government applied the biggest deflationary cuts since 1949, plus a raise in taxes - particularly through Callaghan's new Selective Employment Tax.

Continued economic problems were accompanied by the highest unemployment figures since 1940, and a freeze on wages. Devaluation had to occur, and it finally came in November 1967. Callaghan resigned, and was succeeded by Roy Jenkins, who showed himself to be cautious in developing economic policy and applying what were regarded as strict controls. Jenkins had the advantage of not being stuck with Callaghan's history of opposition to devaluation, and of being regarded as a professional economist – although his qualification for this was not particularly strong, unlike his rival for the job, Tony Crosland. Yet Jenkins' policies eventually succeeded in producing much more encouraging export figures, and a surplus on the balance of payments, in the nine months before the next General Election.

The Prime Minister sought relief from domestic economic problems by turning to Foreign Policy, where he tried – unsuccessfully – to present himself as peacemaker between the United States and Vietnam, and attempted – equally unsuccessfully – to solve the problems caused by Rhodesia's illegal declaration of independence. There was some opposition within Tory ranks to the government's policies on Rhodesia, but the Leader of the Opposition, Ted Heath, did not join in. Wilson's other Foreign Policy adventure involved an unsuccessful attempt to negotiate entry into the European Economic Community, where he was regarded as stealing Heath's clothes. Emerging problems in Northern Ireland were handled not by Wilson but by Callaghan in his new role as Home Secretary.

Papas in the Guardian *of 23 May 1970 makes the point that eighteen-year-olds are now entitled to vote. More than 450,000 young voters had been added to the Register, but Papas suggests they will not be attracted by what is on offer from Heath and Wilson.*

The impact of low productivity and devaluation meant that the Government suffered criticism both through the higher cost of living, and through its controls over the extent to which wages were allowed to catch up with prices. Wilson remained pragmatic, and perennially optimistic, but his failed attempts to balance right and left wing factions in his government reduced his credibility as Prime Minister. In March 1968 the Foreign Secretary, George Brown, left the government, and although he remained as Deputy Leader of the Labour Party his expressed distaste for Wilson's style of government contributed to a more general view that the government was not being run well. What had started as criticism within Wilson's government and party quickly became more widespread.

Within the Labour government Barbara Castle suffered a serious failure in her attempts to carry through a major reform of industrial relations, expressed in her 1969 White Paper "In Place of Strife". This would have introduced for the first time significant penalties for unions which failed to follow negotiated agreements, or to control unofficial strikes. However, the unions were naturally opposed, the Labour Party in parliament came round to the same position, and eventually a Cabinet majority defeated

Trog's cartoon in the Daily Mail *of 1 June 1970 shows Heath and Wilson interrupted in their Election fight by the realisation that most of the electorate is more interested in the progress of World Cup football. England's first match was to be played the following night, and the tournament would continue throughout the Election campaign.*

John Jensen in the Sunday Telegraph *of 31 May 1970, and Kenneth Mahood in* Punch *of 10 June 1970, both attack the sterile point-scoring between Wilson and Heath over the past record of their parties.*

The Grave Diggers

THE FIRE FIGHTER

Tony Benn's attack on Powell's "evil, filthy and obscene" comments was portrayed in John Jensen's cartoon "The Fire Fighter" in the Sunday Telegraph of 7 June 1970. However, Jensen suggests that in fact Benn's attempt to blow out the flames of "Powellism" is only raising them higher.

"Bad? Oh no, my dear, we're good in parts!"

In the Daily Express of 8 June 1970, Cummings showed major figures in the Labour government as rotten eggs - referring to Gerald du Maurier's classic 1895 Punch cartoon, in which a mild curate with a bad boiled egg insists that "parts of it are excellent." Wilson, Callaghan and Jenkins are bad eggs giving off peculiar odours, while the much smaller Benn has exploded with his comparison of Powell and the Nazis. Crossman is also giving off odours, whilst Brown has of course exploded already.

her proposals. A further government failure was its unsuccessful attempt to reform the House of Lords - prevented by the extraordinary partnership of Enoch Powell and the left-wing Michael Foot.

As Leader of the Opposition, Ted Heath also tried to secure balance within his party. For the first time in twenty years he encouraged significant work on alternative policies, although at the time these were portrayed as seriously right wing, particularly by opponents. Even more crucially Heath took what can be seen as one of the most demonstrative actions by a modern political leader when, in April 1968, he dismissed Enoch Powell from the shadow cabinet for his speech attacking immigration. Nevertheless, Powell's reputation for both logic and moral rectitude, combined with his ability to produce populist imagery, left him a significant body of support among the electorate.

Election Issues and the 1970 Election Campaign

The General Election was called for 18 June 1970. Campaigning was made easy by extraordinarily fine weather, but despite the rhetoric on both sides there were few excitements during the campaign. There were some references to the problems in Ulster and to the Common Market - all three parties agreeing on negotiating entry if "the terms were right". There was also debate about which party - if either - would introduce a further wage freeze, and Heath tried to focus on price rises by describing the whole event as a "Shopping basket election". Yet on the whole the campaign was once again considered rather dull.

This dullness was afterwards attributed to Wilson's simple strategy of projecting his own and his government's competence, rather than proposing significant new policies. Yet there were few fundamental issues around which the Labour and Conservative parties could have fought the campaign. In the absence of policies the focus on the leaders was

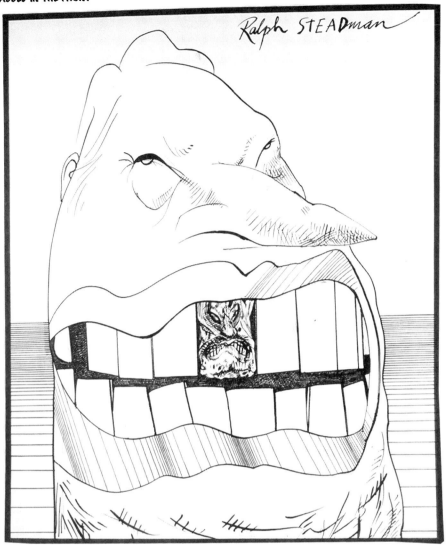

Ralph STEADman

The 1970 Election campaign was the first in which the Times had employed a political cartoonist, and their choice of Ralph Steadman was an interesting one. This savage image of Heath, with small eyes and bloated features, and with Enoch Powell as the rotten tooth in his broad grin, appeared on 20 June 1970.

greater than ever. Despite some evidence to the contrary, Wilson was still seen as the master of public relations. He could deliver effective speeches, and successfully manipulate hecklers, whilst Heath was regarded as relatively wooden and unpersuasive. The new Liberal leader, Jeremy Thorpe, came across as energetic and seemed modern through his use of a helicopter.

Since the newspapers found Heath dull and Wilson predictable, they were happy to focus on the strong personality of Enoch Powell. In his election address he urged the policy of "halt immigration now", but it is not clear whether this speech - or a subsequent one in which Powell complained over the lack of support given to him by the Tory leadership - helped or hindered Conservative electoral prospects. Heath would not disavow Powell as a candidate, but he was attacked by Labour's Tony Benn, who declared that "the flag of racialism which has been hoisted in Wolverhampton is beginning to look like the one that fluttered twenty five years ago over Dachau and Belsen". The papers were largely unsympathetic to Powell, but they also saw Benn as intemperate, and their cartoonists seized on the incident.

As it entered the 1970 Election campaign, Labour seemed to have overcome its three years of governmental disasters. It had lost fifteen by-elections during the parliament, but the polls continued to give Labour a significant lead - until one ominous poll right on the eve of the Election.

'Abominable snowman ?—just another Tory scare, Roy—I promise you !'

In his cartoon "Abominable snowman?" in the Daily Mail *of 9 June 1970, "Emmwood" - John Musgrave-Wood - refers to the previous day's reports of a yeti footprint found on Annapurna. Wilson has discarded his Napoleonic outfit, and basks in the sunny opinion polls with his Chancellor, Roy Jenkins, refusing to believe that there are threats to the benign economic environment.*

Kenneth Baker recalls the 1970 General Election: "At the beginning of 1970 Ted Heath and the Tories had a lead of over twenty points in the opinion polls. Ted had just won the Sydney to Hobart Race and it looked as if the Tories were going to sail into power. But in the following six months Wilson fought back and I remember Minister after Minister coming down to the House of Commons announcing expenditure programmes for any number of activities. When Dick Crossman announced extra money for the London Zoo, Ian McLeod's comment was, "They even haven't forgotten the monkeys".

When the campaign started in June Wilson had a commanding lead and the general assumption was that Labour would win. As the cartoons show, it became a very personal contest between Harold Wilson and Ted Heath. In fact, the campaign had turned to the Tories on the Monday of that week.

I was fighting to hold Acton which I had won in a by-election in 1968. I attended a huge open-air meeting with all the other Conservative candidates on Hounslow Heath in West London at 1.00 pm on the Monday afternoon. Ted Heath arrived standing up in a Land Rover in his shirtsleeves. He had just received the balance of payment figures which showed a huge deficit which he had predicted. This was the evidence he needed to show that the gloss was coming off the Labour record. He was like a man new-born and from that moment the campaign swung in his favour. I didn't hold on to Acton, it returned to the Labour fold, and so I had the unusual and rather unhappy experience of not flowing with the tide."

"Oh dear, the Communists are trying to introduce politics
into the General Election!"

"Oh dear..." by "Eccles" - Frank Brown - in the Morning Star *of 8 June 1970
reinforces the point that to the far left neither Heath nor Wilson were presenting
radical solutions to the nation's problems.*

"JUMP!!"

Paul Rigby's cartoon "Jump!!" in the Sun *of 17 June 1970 portrays the British
electorate as a family trapped in a burning building, uncertain which party will
catch them safely if they jump.*

Personality of the 1970 Election

Enoch Powell

Enoch Powell was Professor of Poetry in Australia at the age of twenty-five, and was subsequently a wartime Brigadier, but this early brilliant success misled him into thinking he would have a similar success in politics. He became an MP for Wolverhampton in 1950, and gradually moved through ministerial jobs until in 1958 he resigned as one of the Prime Minister's Treasury team, a principled act that Macmillan loftily dismissed as a "little local difficulty".

In 1959 Powell added to the moral authority he gained from his resignation by attacking the conduct of a prison camp in Kenya - when that country was still a British responsibility. After two years on the back benches he returned as a successful Minister of Health, entering the Cabinet in 1962 but leaving it again the following year, with a principled refusal to serve under Macmillan's successor, Sir Alec Douglas Home. After 1964 Powell's continuing strong self-belief caused him to take a different view from his shadow cabinet colleagues on a number of issues, and when in 1965 he stood against Heath and Maudling for the Conservative leadership, he secured only fifteen votes.

In 1968, Powell made a speech on immigration which gained him more notoriety than fame. He claimed that the British people would be wrong to permit further immigration, and made a classical allusion - obscure to most of his supporters - to the river Tiber foaming with blood. Heath sacked him from the shadow cabinet for the general tenor and exaggeration of his speech, and Powell never returned to the Front Bench. Further speeches in 1970 were of doubtful help to the Conservative election success.

Though Powell's economic beliefs were similar to those later developed by Margaret Thatcher, his opposition to Heath and the Conservative Party over Europe caused him in February 1974 to recommend a vote against Heath's Government. Powell finished his political career passionately defending the rights of Ulster Unionists. He had a capacity for populist phrase making, and a reputation for moral certitude combined with logic, but with hindsight his comment that "all political careers end in failure" is compelling.

Powell appears again in Nicholas Garland's Daily Telegraph *cartoon of 15 June 1970. The previous day's papers had reported his fulminations against "the enemy within" - a shadowy alliance including protestors and coloured immigrants - and Garland shows Wilson saying to Callaghan "You can see what he means..." as Powell puts an own goal past Anthony Barber as Conservative goalkeeper. The other team members are Home, Macleod, Maudling, Heath and Hogg.*

"You can see what he means when he says beware the enemy within!"

The Result of the 1970 General Election

At 72% of the electorate, the turnout in 1970 was the lowest for thirty five years. The result was:

Conservative	330	46.4%
Labour	287	43.0%
Liberal	6	7.5%
Other	7	3.1%

The Labour vote was down by nearly one million, and Wilson subsequently tried to claim that it was affected by West Germany's World Cup defeat of England four days before the poll. This was a significant event, given England's high hopes after beating West Germany to win the World Cup in 1966, but there is no serious evidence that it influenced the vote. Other critics blamed a relatively complacent campaign by Wilson, which did nothing to overcome a significant period of failure by his government.

The Cartoonist of the 1970 Election

Australia has contributed more expatriate cartoonists to the British press than any other country. John Jensen was born in Sydney, and his first published work appeared in local newspapers, but in 1950 he left Australia for London. From 1953 Jensen was a contributor to *Punch*, and his work covered a wide variety of subjects, but in 1961 he became the first ever political cartoonist on the *Sunday Telegraph*.

Many cartoonists' style varies during their lifetime, but Jensen is unusual in experimenting with a number of different styles at the same time. This can make his cartoons much less immediately recognisable, but the lack of predictability can also be a strength. This is true of his work during the 1970 General Election, as shown in the cartoons selected for this book.

In the course of a conversation with this author, Jensen was asked whether British political cartoons have become more savage since he first arrived in London. His reply was that although the drawings were then less blunt and brutal, the ideas behind the cartoons were as incisive as they are now. Jensen's cartoon "The Fire Fighter" in the *Sunday Telegraph* of 7 June 1970 can be seen in terms of these comments. Here Jensen is pointing out that although Enoch Powell is a frightening figure, it was Benn's speech that had fanned the flames.

Chapter 9
Who Governs Britain?

'I'M NOT SURE THAT 'WHO GOVERNS BRITAIN?' IS A QUESTION WE SHOULD DRAW ATTENTION TO!'

Nicholas Garland's New Statesman cartoon of 18 January 1974 is a bleak representation of a country beset by inflation, unemployment, strikes, and a three-day week. In the days before the Election is called, Ted Heath walks through the chaos, suggesting to his Employment Secretary, Willie Whitelaw, that "Who Governs Britain?" may prove an embarrassing question. Lord Carrington - Secretary of State for Energy, and Anthony Barber - Chancellor of the Exchequer, tag along behind.

The Run-up to the February 1974 General Election

Ted Heath's unexpected success in winning the 1970 Election was followed by a whole series of policy initiatives and changes. The most far-reaching of these was his agreement with France over Britain's joining the Common Market. The necessary Bill passed through Parliament, creating splits on both Conservative and Labour sides, and Heath signed the Treaty of Accession in January 1972. In terms of his subsequent reputation, Britain's entry into the Common Market led to the identification of Heath with a major change in British history, although over the next thirty years this change became increasingly suspect in his own party.

One of Margaret Thatcher's most memorable speeches, in which she declined to engage in "U-turns" was a direct reference to the fact that Heath's Government had changed its policies in major ways. These changes could be seen as sensible reactions to events – but they can also be seen as a failure of nerve. In particular, the domestic policies of Heath's government have not received much praise from objective historians, let alone from his successors in the Tory Party leadership. His government first pursued an anti-inflationary policy without any controls, then a growth policy, then a statutory policy controlling prices and incomes. The 1972 Industrial Relations Act - the first major intervention in trade union affairs since 1926 - created antagonism with the trade unions, and yet its requirement for strike ballots and cooling-off periods seemed to lead to little that was positive.

Garland is one of the few modern cartoonists happy to use literary allusions, and his cartoon "I knew him Horatio…", from the New Statesman of 8 February 1974, carries references to Act V of Hamlet. Barber is drawn as Horatio, Heath is Hamlet himself, and Yorick's skull has become Stage III of the Statutory Incomes Policy, which was due to start at the end of the year, but was perhaps better buried.

" I KNEW HIM HORATIO; A FELLOW OF INFINITE JEST, OF MOST EXCELLENT FANCY; HE HATH BORNE ME ON HIS BACK A THOUSAND TIMES; AND NOW, HOW ABHORRED IN MY IMAGINATION IT IS! MY GORGE RISES AT IT."

After its Election defeat the Labour Party devoted a lot of time to internal battles, rather than to fighting the Conservative government. Wilson's great tactical skills sustained his leadership, for it was readily apparent that no other major figure on the Labour front bench could keep the party together over Europe, or, subsequently, could successfully reduce the party's manifesto commitment to extended public ownership. However, the Wilson governments were accused of lacking both direction and socialist virtues, and two of Wilson's colleagues moved in opposite political directions. Anthony Wedgwood Benn became a fervent advocate of increased socialism and greater democracy within the Labour Party, whilst Michael Foot - the stereotype firebrand left-wing orator - for the first time took responsibility on the Labour front bench.

The Labour Shadow Cabinet somehow seemed to contain more powerful and interesting characters than did the Heath Cabinet, which was weakened in July 1970 by the early death of Iain Macleod. However, dissatisfaction with the Conservative government was expressed less in a

Cummings' cartoon in the Daily Express of 8 February 1974 shows Heath, Barber, and the emollient Secretary of State for Employment, Willie Whitelaw, charging the enemy guns as if in the disastrous Charge of the Light Brigade. The cannons are to be fired from the left by Jeremy Thorpe, Enoch Powell, Harold Wilson, Mick McGahey - Communist Vice President of the Mineworkers, Joe Gormley - President of the NUM, and Laurence Daly - General Secretary of the NUM.

move to Labour than through an upsurge of Liberal support, especially at by-elections. Heath appointed one woman Cabinet Minister – Margaret Thatcher, who was responsible for Education. Her habit of wearing colourful hats ensured that she received attention from cartoonists.

In January 1972 the first national coal strike for almost fifty years had introduced the country to flying pickets, extending the impact of the strike to other industries. In November 1973 an overtime ban by the miners led to the declaration of a state of emergency. The government was also faced with rising oil prices - the economic consequences of the Arab/Israeli War of October 1973 - and responded by imposing a three-day working week throughout industry and commerce. Prices and wages chased each other upwards, and there was widespread feeling that the government was not in control, even before the final impact of a new miners' strike in February 1974. The government had delegated responsibility for decisions about prices and incomes to statutory boards, and the miners were seen as attempting to destroy the government which had introduced these statutory controls.

On 7 February Heath called a General Election for 28 February 1974. The 10.30 pm curfew that had been imposed on television broadcasts, because of the electricity shortages, was lifted for the duration of the campaign.

"Eccles" - Frank Brown - in the Morning Star *of 11 February 1974 attacks Heath with a parody of the Conservative campaigning slogan "Who's Running Britain?".*

"They'll promise you anything to get in!"

Two cartoons by "Jak" - Raymond Jackson - from the Evening Standard *of 11 February and 28 February 1974, suggest a lack of faith in the three Party leaders. The first cartoon depicts them on identical posters - trying to appear Churchillian - and the second shows them making identical appeals for forgiveness. Jak has captured Thorpe's face brilliantly, and the presence of a teddy bear in his bed is intriguing – perhaps relating to some early gossip about his sexual inclinations.*

"...and forgive me for all the fibs I've told, and all the promises I've made...!"

"Just leave it all to old Mr Fixit, sonny, there's NOTHING he can't do!"

Paul Rigby's cartoon "Just leave it to old Mr Fixit", in the Sun *of 13 February 1974, casts a jaundiced eye on Harold Wilson's power over the unions. While the miners continued on strike, Wilson had managed to persuade the smaller ASLEF rail union to halt its industrial action, which began the previous month.*

Election Issues and the February 1974 Election Campaign

The Prime Minister may have decided the date of the Election, but it was the miners who brought it about. Attempts to persuade them to call off their strike during the Election campaign failed, although they did not engage in the mass picketing which had been so vivid a feature of the 1972 strike. Wilson and Jeremy Thorpe denounced the Election as unnecessary and unhelpful in settling the miners' strike, but Heath claimed that he needed a fresh mandate for dealing with the strike and other issues. He saw the Election as being fought over the question of "Who governs Britain".

The impact of inflation was shown in a record rise in prices reported during the Election campaign, and all three parties were agreed that the control of inflation was of prime concern. They differed on how to achieve it - Labour proposed to do so by controlling prices but seeking only a voluntary agreement on wages, in contrast to both the Conservatives and Liberals who believed in the need for statutory controls. During the Election, people showed they were more interested in the cost of living than anything else, although they had no strong belief that either Labour or Conservative would control these costs effectively. The press portrayed the country as in crisis – a not unreasonable conclusion in the circumstance of a three-day week.

In attacking the government, Labour repeatedly pointed to the 35% increase in prices since it left office in June 1970, and in his speeches Wilson made use of Cummings' 1950s cartoon character by talking about the need to "Get rid of Mr Rising Price". He also declared the virtues of a "social contract" he claimed to have agreed with the unions, although there were no details of what this actually involved. Wilson also managed to keep the majority of his Party together by adopting a more critical position on the Common Market. Labour's policy was now to renegotiate the terms on which the country had entered Europe, and to have a referendum on the results.

Labour was not very successful in pushing Europe to the forefront of the Election campaign, but this was achieved by Enoch Powell with two speeches towards the end of February 1974. In the first he inveighed against the whole process of joining Europe, and the way in which this had been

Emmwood's cartoon in the Daily Mail *of 19 February 1974 shows Wilson disguised with a wolf's skin to scare the electorate with rising prices, unaware that the real wolf of inflation lurks behind. Emmwood is suggesting that voters should be more scared of Wilson than they are - a nice idea, if a rather confused presentation.*

done. In the second - on 25 February - he took his opposition even further, advising Tories who wanted to vote against the Common Market to vote Labour, as he said he would do. The Liberal Party, which had been advancing through the previous two years, meanwhile continued to show the potential of a high Liberal vote, which sustained the belief that voting Liberal was not necessarily a waste of a vote.

The issue of the miners loomed large in the first week of the campaign, and then reappeared in the closing stages, when it seemed possible that there had been errors in calculating what they were actually being paid, suggesting that a larger increase might be justified.

Cummings in the Daily Express *of 25 February 1974 shows Jeremy Thorpe as Justice, holding Heath and Wilson in his scales, but unaware that he in turn is held in the balance by Joe Gormley, President of the National Union of Mineworkers. At this stage neither the Conservative nor Labour Parties had attempted any sort of deal with the Liberals – though they had refrained from attacking them.*

In February 1974 **Jim Callaghan** was both Shadow Foreign Secretary and Chairman of the Labour Party. He returned from a visit to Jerusalem when the Election was called, and remembers what followed: "For three weeks I travelled the country addressing meetings in Lancashire, the Midlands, the Home Counties and the South Wales Valleys; Cardiff, my constituency, did not see much of me. Even so, my majority was larger than previously, which led my Agent (cynical as the breed always is) to say that the more I stayed away at election time from Cardiff, the better the results he could achieve.

The pattern of activity rarely varied. In the morning, an early strategy meeting at Transport House in London, followed by a Press Conference (more for the benefit of underemployed Lobby Correspondents than of enlightenment to the voter), then a dash by train or car to undertake a provincial tour with a midnight, or later, return to London.

Nearly every day, I and others came back with reports of large, well attended meetings and considerable enthusiasm, and Labour activists in much better heart than in 1970. Yet the opinion polls were all showing a big majority for the Conservative Government and we tended to believe the pollsters rather than our own experiences.

When Mr Heath did not at once resign, Harold Wilson wanted to denounce it as constitutionally improper. It was not, and at a Shadow Cabinet meeting on the day after polling, I argued strongly that it would be better for the public to see Ted Heath as a bad loser, rather than set a constitutional hare running. Harold reluctantly agreed but changed his mind over the weekend and told Percy Clark to arrange for a TV crew to visit him. Percy quite properly reported this to me and I at once countermanded the order. Percy did so and made up some excuse. Three days later Ted Heath resigned. I never told Harold what I had done."

Personality of the February 1974 General Election

Jeremy Thorpe

Jeremy Thorpe was the son and grandson of Conservative MPs, but in 1959 he was elected Liberal MP for North Devon, and in 1967 he succeeded Jo Grimond as Party Leader. In 1968 Thorpe launched the Liberals' "Great Crusade", but a small drop in the Party's national vote in the 1970 General Election meant that it lost half its seats. Yet within two years by-election victories were bringing greater credibility, and in the February 1974 General Election the Liberals won over six million votes - more than at any time since 1926, but still only enough to gain them fourteen seats.

Thorpe had planned the Liberals' successful campaign, and might have been tempted by Heath's offer of a coalition, but his party - eager to gain a promise of proportional representation - was less enthusiastic. This was the peak of Thorpe's career. He was an excellent orator, skilful and witty in debate, and with a reputation for being clever - although perhaps superficial. His famous comment from 1962, when Macmillan sacked a third of his Cabinet, has already been quoted: "Greater love hath no man than this: that he lay down his friends for his life." Unfortunately these verbal skills did not

The Thing in the Middle of the Road

Les Gibbard's cartoon "The Thing in the Middle of the Road", from the Guardian *of 1 March 1974, represents the damage caused to both the Labour and Conservative Election campaigns by the Liberal Party. In securing their 19.1% poll the Liberals had taken a significant number of votes from both Labour and the Tories.*

Trog's cartoon in Punch *for 13 February 1974 suggests that although Wilson was aiming his tax policies at the upper class, they would actually hit the middle classes. Wilson makes a stocky Robin Hood, while in the background his band of outlaws comprises Tony Benn as Friar Tuck, Ted Short - Labour's Deputy Leader, a delicate looking Shirley Williams and Jim Callaghan.*

TARGET PRACTICE

Paul Rigby's deliberately-crowded cartoon in the Sun *for Election Day - 28 February 1974 - illustrates the army of problems that awaited the next occupant of 10 Downing Street.*

appeal to cartoonists, who focused more on Thorpe's somewhat cadaverous features.

In 1976 Thorpe had to resign the Party Leadership because of allegations about a homosexual relationship. This scandal finally resulted in a charge of conspiracy to murder, but he was acquitted in 1979, shortly after losing his seat in the General Election. These circumstances, unique among leaders of British political parties, gave an especially sad conclusion to his political career.

The Result of the February 1974 General Election

Just as in 1970, the pre-election polls were misleading, as they forecast a Conservative victory. There was a larger turnout than in the 1970 General Election - 78.1% of the electorate - but Labour still gained power with a smaller share of the poll than in previous post-war elections where it had been defeated. The final result was:

Labour	301	37.1%
Conservative	297	37.8%
Liberals	14	19.3%
Welsh & Scottish Nationalists	9	2.6%
Others	14	3.2%

This was the first General Election since 1929 which failed to produce a clear majority for one party, and Heath did not resign for four days in the hope of securing a coalition with the Liberals.

The Cartoonist of the February 1974 Election

Les Gibbard, who succeeded Bill Papas as political cartoonist on the Guardian, is a New Zealander - one of many expatriate cartoonists to work for British newspapers. Gibbard's cartoons of the February 1974 General Election are very representative of his style, in which small figures battle against the hard realities of politics.

Cartooning mythology has it that the giants of political cartooning constantly make newspaper readers gnash their teeth, reach for their fountain pens and threaten to cancel their subscriptions, but this is not Gibbard's view. "I am afraid we political cartoonists tend to preach to the converted", he has explained: "Cabinet Ministers may read the Guardian but not many Tory voters do. It therefore follows that no matter how clever a cartoon may have been and how irrefutable its logic, it has never made one iota of difference to the outcome of a poll".

Chapter 10
Vote for Peace and Quiet

"Miners more...pensioners more..." by "Jak" - Raymond Jackson - was published in the Evening Standard *on 16 September 1974, two days before the Election date was announced. Wilson - in characteristic cartoon outfit of pipe and Gannex raincoat - runs through the Labour Manifesto with Barbara Castle, Jim Callaghan, a doubtful Roy Jenkins and Michael Foot.*

" Miners more . . . pensioners more . . . dentists more . . . nurses more — now you're sure we haven't left anyone out just before the election? "

The Run-up to the October 1974 General Election

The General Election of February 1974 had failed to produce a clear majority, and Labour took power in the knowledge that a second General Election could not be far ahead. In fact the Parliament that followed was the shortest for almost three hundred years.

Harold Wilson took office without an overall majority, but he did not repeat Ted Heath's failed attempt to negotiate an understanding or coalition with the Liberal Party. He preferred to govern as though he had a majority, and in fact none of the other parties saw any advantage in bringing down the Labour government. During its short life the Labour government did manage to settle the miners' strike, repeal the 1972 Industrial Relations Act, and increase pensions. Meanwhile the country faced increasing economic problems, with an eight percent increase in prices and a sixteen percent increase in wages during the life of the government, plus an even further decline in the balance of payments figures.

Wilson continued to demonstrate his short-term tactical skills by setting up a Cabinet that was balanced between left and right. Tony Benn, as Secretary of State for Industry, continued to press for a more Socialist policy - his proposals including further public ownership and "planning agreements" with companies receiving government money - but Wilson toned down these proposals, and the eventual Labour Manifesto made no specific commitments on these issues. Michael Foot's apotheosis continued with his appointment as Secretary of State for Employment, and the Chancellor of the Exchequer, Denis Healey, managed to produce two slightly contradictory budgets.

For its part the Conservative opposition entered no defence of the 1972 Industrial Relations Act - despite the fact that two years earlier it had been one of their major innovations. Since open confrontation with the miners had not worked, Heath's new style was one of moderation, in the hope that this would bring back Tory voters and attract Liberals. Enoch Powell's power to disrupt was no longer so significant - he was not an MP or even a candidate until the last moment, and then it was not for the Conservative Party but for the Ulster Unionists.

When Parliament adjourned for the Summer in July 1974 no one expected it to meet again.

The theme of promises was also chosen by "Emmwood" - John Musgrave-Wood - for his Daily Mail *cartoon of 19 September 1974. In a parody of a music-hall bill the words have become the most significant feature of the cartoon - and Wilson is drawn as the music-hall comedian George Robey, known as "The Prime Minister of Mirth". The merciful shortness of the Election campaign is noted at the bottom.*

"Trust us, Britannia, to lead you through the night of inflation . . ."

Cummings' cartoon in the Daily Express *on the day the election was announced - 18 September 1974 - shows Wilson leading an equally blindfolded and stumbling Benn and Healey followed by a bewildered Britannia. Their futile guiding light is the "Social Contract" - an agreement that a Labour government would introduce measures of social benefit in return for a reduction in unions' demands for wages.*

Election Issues and the October 1974 Campaign

On 18 September the General Election was announced for 10 October 1974. It was to be a relatively short campaign, although the competition for votes lacked the vigour and immediacy of the February 1974 General Election, with its air of crisis. The strengths of the major contestants, Wilson and Heath, were after all well recognised, as were their weaknesses – Heath's cold public personality being balanced in de-merit by Wilson's tendency to exaggerate and sensationalise.

The Labour government had not been in power long enough to be blamed for inflation, but Denis Healey's attempt to prove that it was not really as bad as people thought - telling one press conference that it was "only 8.4%" - was regarded as a bad mistake. Luckily for Healey, Heath's response was treated as equally bogus, and it seems likely that the Conservative Party was still blamed for the declining economic situation. Labour decided against giving Tony Benn a prominent role in the Election campaign, although the Conservatives still pointed to his passionate advocacy of Socialism as evidence that the Labour leadership was in thrall to the left wing - a situation for which Benn may privately have wished.

Labour made much greater use of Shirley Williams - the epitome of reasonableness. However, she created one of the few sensations in the Election campaign by giving a straight answer to a direct question. Asked what she would do if the public voted against the Common Market in a referendum, she said that she would leave politics. Roy Jenkins, who early

Les Gibbard in the Guardian of 30 September 1974 shows a bewildered voter trying to listen to the three party leaders at once, as they try to sell him their unappealing cars. The third car is labelled "Hard Ride", for the supposedly middle of the road Liberals were in fact offering a rather tough approach to issues.

"Mrs Williams! Mr Jenkins! If you utter that smear-word again we shall have to expel you, too, from the Union!"

in the campaign had pressed for Labour to take account of moderate opinion, then admitted that he would leave the Cabinet if an anti-Europe decision emerged. The principled stand taken by Williams and Jenkins was contrasted unfavourably with the shifting policy of the Labour Party, in opposition and in government.

Wilson's success in moderating left-wing influence in the Cabinet and in the House of Commons, and in presenting the Labour government as serious and responsible, was reinforced by his own plea that the electorate should be given a period of "peace and quiet" - although this was a long way from the white heat of technological revolution he had advocated ten years earlier. Not surprisingly, the Conservatives decided against presenting themselves as a reborn party with new ideas, and Heath fell back on the old Conservative staple of an appeal for National Unity. Yet the phrase had no meaning unless he could reach an agreement with one or more of the other parties, and only at the very last moment did he make a serious effort to achieve this. Apart from this vague appeal to unity, the main effort to persuade people to vote Conservative was made by an increasingly prominent Margaret Thatcher, who promised that mortgages would be cut to 9.5%.

Cummings's cartoon "Mrs Williams! Mr Jenkins!" in the Daily Express *of 27 September 1974 refers to the public position on the Common Market taken first by Shirley Williams, and then by Roy Jenkins. When asked at a Labour press conference what she would do if the country voted "No", Williams ignored Wilson's efforts to stifle the question and answered "I should not remain in active politics". Benn, Wilson and Foot have become the union committee, and Denis Healey as Chancellor waits to collect the fines.*

Acupuncture anaesthesia: "Then on the tenth, one of us, or two of us, or three of us, will start operating on you"

THE INCOMPARABLE ILLINGWORTH

On 22 September 1974, Leslie Illingworth - now guest cartoonist on the News of the World - *showed the three leaders as acupuncturists treating "Johnny Bull" for inflation. Wilson seems unusually benign, whilst Thorpe seems almost to be tickling the patient — as he often did through his witty contributions to debate.*

John Jensen's cartoon "A Party Political Broadcast" in the Sunday Telegraph *of 29 September 1974, comments on the similarity between the television broadcasts of all three major parties. Party Political Broadcasts were carried simultaneously on all three television channels, and were well established as a significant formative influence on voting behaviour.*

The Labour government might have been damaged by "the slag heaps affair" - a financial scandal that now seems very moderate, but which involved a promising mixture of the Prime Minister's secretary's brother, a land reclamation scheme, and Labour Party dominance in the northeast. Luckily the case did not come to court until after the General Election, and the whiff of corruption did not become a major feature in the campaign. In the following year David Butler and Dennis Kavanagh concluded in their book on the October 1974 Election that "corruption is not readily exploited as an electoral theme in British politics" - later campaigns would present a different picture.

"Coalition? NEVER! We don't need to join anybody!"

On 3 October 1974 Paul Rigby's cartoon "Coalition? NEVER!" in the Sun *showed senior Labour politicians in the pocket of the trade unions - Wilson being chained to Foot on one side, and Benn and Healey on the other, whilst a hammer and sickle decorates the watch fob. Heath appears as a two-faced suitor, on one side rejected by Wilson, and on the other received coldly by Thorpe - looking even more cadaverous than usual.*

Jim Prior, a senior member of Heath's Shadow Cabinet, recalls the October 1974 General Election: "This was never going to be an easy election for the Conservative Party. Defeated in March, the odds on a much greater defeat in October were easy to calculate. The tactics of the Labour Government in the interim period were to do as little as possible to upset the electorate. Trade Unions were bought off with beneficial legislation, VAT was reduced and hopefully the economy would survive until after an election which would produce a healthy majority, and a safe return to power. It didn't quite turn out as expected, and Labour's overall majority was wafer thin. This proved to be too small for an effective government even though Liberal support was forthcoming.

Despite deep gloom in the Conservative Party, they hit upon two policies which proved very popular with the voters – they were the abolition of domestic rates and pegging mortgage rate to a maximum of 9.5%. Significantly it was a slightly-reluctant Margaret Thatcher to whom fell the task of promoting these policies and she did it very well.

With the inestimable benefit of hindsight it is easy to recognise that both major parties over-committed themselves, thereby causing endless trouble thereafter. These were very difficult days for any government with Britain regarded - with some justification - as the "sick man of Europe", and it was this depressing scene which led the Conservatives to call for a government of national unity without having much idea as to how it would work in practice. It would be a further five years before reality took over and the country was restored once more to sanity."

Heath's contrasting approaches to the General Elections of February and October 1974 is the subject of "A Man for All Seasons" by "Eccles" - Frank Brown - in the Morning Star *of 1 October 1974. The difference is shown as much in Heath's face as in the more obvious spiked club and bouquet.*

A Man For All Seasons

9—15 OCTOBER 1974   20p WEEKLY

Punch

TED HEATH:
Final Appearance—
or Grand Comeback?

The image of the face behind the mask had been used before, to show one politician being manipulated by another, but for the Punch *cover of 9 October 1974 "Trog" applied it to Heath himself. The cartoon successfully captures Heath's different moods, and suggests that the public change from stern confrontation to friendly conciliation was mask not substance.*

Personality of the October 1974 General Election

Tony Benn

By October 1974 Tony Benn was established as an attractive target for cartoonists - a wild and demonic left-winger, rather like Nye Bevan, complete with staring eyes to represent his supposed fanaticism. His transition from the public school and Oxford educated Anthony Wedgwood Benn, to plain Tony Benn has been presented both as sinister and as risible. When first elected as MP for Bristol in 1950 he announced that he had to lose the stigma of being an intellectual, to which his mentor, Tony Crosland, replied "You'd better acquire the stigma before worrying about losing it."

In 1960 Benn was obliged to resign his Commons seat on the death of his father, Viscount Stansgate, but he fought a prolonged and eventually successful battle for the right to disclaim this title and sit again as an MP, and finally succeeded in 1963. His enemies might indeed contend that his greatest contribution to the Labour Party lay in assisting Alec Douglas Home to renounce his own peerage and become Tory leader, thus helping Harold Wilson to win the election of 1964.

When Benn entered Wilson's government in 1964 he seemed more interested in technology than ideology, but later declared that it was ministerial experience which "really made me into a Socialist in middle-age." While personally courteous and disavowing personal attacks on his opponents, Benn did not enjoy the support among Labour MPs that he had amongst ordinary members, and became identified as an extremist in all the positions he took up. Wilson's feelings about this second transformation were that Benn "immatures with age".

Despite the 1963 Peerage Act, Benn's most significant constitutional contribution was his later persuasion of Wilson's Shadow Cabinet to adopt a referendum on the Common Market - a totally novel approach in the United Kingdom. This is likely to have fewer critics among historians than his internal pursuits of enhanced Socialism, or his version of increased democracy in the Labour Party after 1979. Benn would have transformed the Labour Party into a Socialist Party quite prepared to carry through the rhetoric of its earlier days, but it was gradually recognised that his answer to Thatcherism was not going to win over the electorate. Ironically, some of the democratic reforms he encouraged within the Labour Party subsequently ensured the success of John Smith and Tony Blair.

In his 10 October 1974 cartoon in the Daily Express, *Cummings used the more traditional cartoonist's image of the mask, to show an extremist concealed behind a more moderate exterior. Here a devilish Benn - complete with horns, hooves, tail and convenient label - lurks behind Wilson's Gannex mackintosh and mask. To this Cummings has added another stock image of the political cartoonist, the hidden dangers of the ballot box - in this case with reference to Wilson's suggestion that the electors wanted only peace and quiet.*

*On 6 October 1974 Cummings'
cartoon in the* Sunday Express
*represented the idea that a vote for
the Liberals would in fact be a vote
for Labour. Wilson is a postman
with his sack waiting to collect the
mail from a post-box with Jeremy
Thorpe's face.*

The Results of the October 1974 General Election

The final result of the October 1974 General Election was that Labour
secured an overall majority of three seats. The turnout dropped to 72.8%
of the electorate, from 78.1% eight months earlier. The age of the register
may have contributed to this, but boredom also played a part. The results
were:

Labour	319	39.2%
Conservative	277	35.8%
Liberals	13	18.3%
Other	26	6.7%

The "other" figure included 11 Scottish Nationalists and 3 Plaid Cymru.

The Cartoonist of the October 1974 Election

Nicholas Garland studied at the Slade School of Fine Art, before working for some years as stage manager at the Royal Court Theatre. After contributing drawings to a number of publications, and helping create the "Barrie Mackenzie" strip for *Private Eye* in 1964, he joined the *Daily Telegraph* in 1966 as its first political cartoonist.

At the time of the October 1974 General Election, Garland was drawing cartoons for both the *New Statesman* and the *Daily Telegraph*. His style was reminiscent of Vicky, and he acknowledged both Vicky and Low as major influences - particularly in their focus on ridicule. His cartoons applied that ridicule through a wide variety of references and allusions, not only to films, books, plays, fables, and paintings, but also to the work of other cartoonists.

In 1986 Garland left the *Daily Telegraph* to join the newly-founded *Independent*, but in 1991 returned to the *Daily Telegraph* as political cartoonist. Here he continues to take his ideas from many sources, drawing inspiration from newspapers and television, and also from the editorial conference which he attends frequently. As Garland explains, he is interested in getting the leader writers' "take" on events, though he does not feel led by their opinions. He gives only his final cartoon to the editor, and although he might have discussed ideas with him he does not offer a range of possibilities or rough drafts.

Garland feels very much part of a tradition of cartooning within a climate of political freedom, and emphasises the significance of laughing at politicians. Like Vicky, his cartoons are quite frequently sombre and solemn, particularly in the aftermath of a tragedy or atrocity. Yet on the whole he believes mockery to be more damaging than abuse, and still wonders how effective some of the more grotesque cartoons may be.

Chapter 11
"No Woman in My Time."

In his Daily Express cartoon of 30 March 1979 - "My God! It's about time…" - Michael Cummings looked forward to Margaret Thatcher as the first woman Prime Minister, in a cartoon that advertised her as a careful and conscientious driver for No.10.

"My God! It's about time it had a woman driver!"

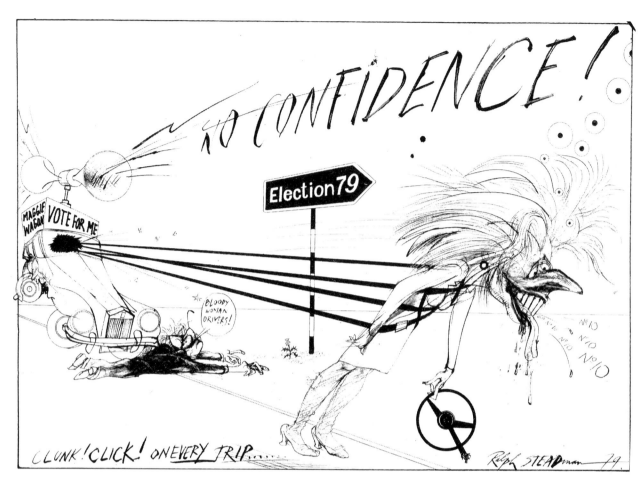

The Run-up to the 1979 General Election

The Labour government elected in October 1974 carried its small minority with increasing weariness through what must have seemed a repetition of history - though this time as tragedy not farce. Constant industrial confrontation, not just over pay, produced screaming headlines in newspapers. The government worked hard to secure a voluntary Incomes Policy, but this provided a temporary sticking plaster for inflation rather than a cure. Economic difficulties obliged it to rely on help from the International Monetary Fund, which in turn led to a substantial programme of deflation. Denis Healey, Chancellor of the Exchequer, presided over a programme of de facto monetarism, which with hindsight has many similarities to that adopted under Margaret Thatcher.

In 1975 the government organised a referendum on membership of the Common Market - Tony Benn's constitutional initiative. This was accompanied by a further unique phenomenon, in the form of an agreement that Cabinet members could take different sides on the issue, and the outcome in favour of Europe also meant that the earlier threats by Shirley Williams and Roy Jenkins did not need to be fulfilled. The question of membership was only temporarily put to bed, but it became an issue within the Conservative and Labour Parties rather than between them. At the same time major steps were taken towards devolving legislative responsibilities in Scotland and Wales, although these proposals were not actually implemented.

Harold Wilson had long been paranoid about supposed attempts to replace him, but in 1976 he removed the cause of the paranoia by suddenly resigning as Prime Minister. He was bored and not physically well, and

Ralph Steadman's cover for the New Statesman *of the same day, 30th March 1979, could scarcely be in greater contrast, for here Thatcher is manic, and the vehicle has become her personal "Maggie Wagon". Slavering with ambition, she is hurtling toward No.10, projected through the windscreen after crashing into James Callaghan as he reaches for the Scottish thistle. The title - "Clunk! Click! On every trip..." - refers to the current road safety seatbelt campaign*

REVIVAL OF MICKEY MOUSE

Stanley Franklin's cartoon "Revival of Mickey Mouse" in the Sun *of 2 April 1979 unusually focuses on the Liberal Party - with David Steel as Mickey Mouse. Cyril Smith pirouettes, whilst Jeremy Thorpe plays the pipes of Pan – although in fact he played no major role in this Election.*

seemed extremely pleased to be able to surprise almost everyone with his resignation. Jim Callaghan - who had restored his reputation by an effective period as Foreign Secretary - beat the left wing Michael Foot to succeed Wilson as Prime Minister. It said something about how left wing the Labour Party had become even in the House of Commons that Michael Foot, the left wing orator and Party conscience, should have so far adapted himself to the realities of government as to be a credible candidate. Roy Jenkins, who won only fifty-six votes in the contest for succession, disappeared to run the European Commission in Brussels.

The Election defeat also brought changes in the Conservative party, where Ted Heath was persuaded to offer himself for re-election as leader. Having lost three Elections, and with few people personally attached to him, he found himself - to his everlasting astonishment - replaced by Margaret Thatcher. It was an amazing outcome, for Mrs Thatcher was the first woman to lead a British political party, and even by the standards of the time the Conservative Party was still extremely prejudiced about the role of women in public life. Her own opinion just fourteen years earlier was that "no woman in my time will be Prime

KEITH WAITE ON SUNDAY

"If you must have a Conservative Prime Minister, I'm your man."

Keith Waite's cartoon "If you must have a Conservative Prime Minister…", in the Sunday Mirror *of 8 April 1979, is probably the first in a mainstream paper to criticise a Labour Prime Minister for being too Conservative, rather than too left wing. At the table Margaret Thatcher is accompanied by Jim Prior and Willie Whitelaw.*

Minister or Chancellor or Foreign Secretary." Her victory not only indicated significant dissatisfaction with Heath, but was also a tribute to a brilliantly-managed electoral campaign and to her own emerging political qualities.

Callaghan sought to patronise her, but Mrs Thatcher earned respect by fighting back. Her militant tone led one Russian commentator to describe her as "an iron maiden", but her forthright way of speaking concealed a relatively cautious approach, both on tactics and policy. She distanced herself from the corporatist and overspending elements of Heath's government, and yet offered relatively little detail about what she would actually do. Meanwhile the Liberal Party managed to achieve a pact which sustained Labour in government for eighteen months, although it remained unsuccessful in by-elections. David Steel had replaced Thorpe as Liberal leader after the latter's involvement in a sex scandal, and showed he would mean more to history than the MP who made abortion more readily available.

As Keith Waite sees it...

"So you're not voting Labour this time"

"So you're not voting Labour...", by Keith Waite in the Daily Mirror *of 9 April 1979, refers to the possible impact of the Conservative promise that council house tenants would be able to buy the houses in which they livde.*

In the autumn of 1978 Jim Callaghan had the chance of calling a General Election, but decided to put it off to the spring of the following year. With hindsight this was a bad decision, for over the succeeding months Labour's Wages Policy collapsed and there were strikes in the Public Sector

On 11 April 1979 the Daily Express *carried Cummings' cartoon of a genially avuncular Callaghan wooing a young Britannia. As in most of this cartoonists' visions of Labour government, the Prime Minister is accompanied by fearsome left-wing figures - including Tony Benn in Maoist uniform with staring eyes.*

"...and of course, dear, you won't mind my family living with us!"

"Mr. Callaghan! In your heart you know I'm right — you'd be happier in MY party..."

Cummings' Daily Express cartoon of 13 April 1979 - "Mr Callaghan!" - repeated the familiar theme of Jim Callaghan being shackled to a Marxist Labour Party led by Tony Benn. Here Callaghan is branded as "Conservative", whilst Mrs Thatcher completes the paradox by offering him freedom under a banner quoting from the Communist Manifesto. Healey and Foot appear in the garden as gnomes.

- with stark headlines about the unburied dead. Callaghan's calm approach started to look like complacency, and the press accused him of denying that there was a crisis, although this was itself an invention. Finally the government carved its own small niche in history by becoming the first since October 1924 to be forced to resign as a result of a vote in the House of Commons. On the following day - 29 March - Callaghan announced a General Election for 3 May 1979.

Jak's cartoon "And now the end is near..." from the Evening Standard *of 1 May 1979 makes use of "My Way" - the song made famous by Frank Sinatra. Callaghan's Cabinet colleagues are Shirley Williams, Hattersley, Benn, Healey, Foot, David Owen, Jon Silkin and Peter Shore. Tony Benn is drawn characteristically out of step, but strangely with his right foot.*

With acknowledgements to "My Way" and Shapiro Bernstein

"And now the end is near,
And as we face the final curtain . . ."

"ME AND MY SHADOW... "

On 2 May 1979 Franklin's Sun *cartoon "Me and My Shadow" showed Jim Callaghan dressed as the ever-hopeful Mr Micawber from Dickens' David Copperfield, but here casting a shadow in the threatening shape of Tony Benn.*

Election Issues and the 1979 Campaign

The rhetoric of the campaign was that it should be the most bitter since the war, between the most right wing Conservative Party and the most left wing Labour Party since 1945. Certainly the cartoons in Conservative papers rather support this idea. Mrs Thatcher set out her store "I am a conviction politician". It was clear she would make substantial changes particularly on reforming Trade Union relations but basically followed a strategy of attacking the Government. The Conservatives were offering a return to a less corporatist more private enterprise economy, with de-nationalisation or privatisation as it was now called and a forecast of tax cuts. Undoubtedly the Conservatives were making radical noises, while Labour and particularly Jim Callaghan were offering a defensive response; controlling the public statements of Benn and the left wing was insufficient to persuade the electorate that Labour offered a bright future.

Waite's cartoon in the Sunday Mirror *of 6 May 1979 shows senior Conservatives celebrating their Election victory. Margaret Thatcher thanks the Labour left, while Keith Joseph, Willie Whitelaw, Jim Prior, and Edward Heath listen approvingly - and Denis Thatcher stands in the background. This was probably the last time a cartoonist depicted Heath smiling at Thatcher – though not the last in which Denis Thatcher was shown smiling approvingly at his wife.*

KEITH WAITE ON SUNDAY

".. I would particularly like to thank those trade unionists who manned the picket lines so effectively for us last winter."

Margaret Thatcher recalls the 1979 General Election: "When you lead your Party, all Elections are memorable - both victories and defeats (though I never experienced any of those). But the 1979 Election, as most likely even my critics would concede, was probably the most politically significant since the War. It really did result in a change of national direction.

The campaign was unusual from the start because it was precipitated amid scenes of high political drama by a vote of no confidence in the then Labour government. But the oddity then continued. The ordinary train of events is that Oppositions attack governments on their record, and governments defend it and try to attack Oppositions on their intentions. But in this campaign there was very little attention to the record at all, which was recognised as really so bad – strikes, inflation, bankruptcy staved off only by the IMF, and so on – that it was simply indefensible. Instead, the election from the very beginning was about the Opposition – and particularly the Leader of the Opposition. Did we offer hope for a new start? Or were we a risk too far?

Prime Minister Callaghan and his colleagues fought a skilful, negative campaign which was intended to rattle us - and some were rattled. But I resolved from the beginning that I was not going to be deflected from campaigning on what I knew were the really big issues - lower income tax rates, reforming trade union law, restraining the size of the state, widening choice and promoting ownership. As a result, there was a strange, sometimes almost eerie, discontinuity between the daily charges and doomfilled warnings from Labour on the one hand and the broad themes which came out of my speeches and the Conservative election broadcasts on the other.

There were also some lighter moments. One day campaigning in East Anglia for the farming vote, I had to navigate my way boot-less through a field of cows in search of a calf which I was supposed to cradle in my arms. (Such things seem strangely dated now that politics seems to consist in a prolonged contest to demonstrate a cloying degree of touchy-feely soft-heartedness). I was used to babies, but not calves. At one moment, Denis - practical as ever - called out: 'If we're not careful we'll have a dead calf on our hands'. But thankfully it survived my attentions. And, as history records, I too survived the attentions of the Labour Party."

Personalities of the 1979 General Election

Margaret Thatcher

The first woman to lead a British political party, Margaret Thatcher was the daughter of a lower middle class shopkeeper in Grantham. Educated at Oxford University, where she read science, she later became a lawyer, and in 1959 was elected as MP for Finchley. She quickly came to prominence - not only among cartoonists, who were fascinated by the hats she wore at Conservative conferences. As Secretary of State for Education from 1970 onwards, she was criticised as "Margaret Thatcher milk snatcher" for removing the privilege of free milk from some schoolchildren. She also continued the creation of a comprehensive system of education, which paradoxically seemed less contentious to contemporaries than it would in retrospect.

Mrs Thatcher was not vocal in her opposition to Heath's policies, either within the Cabinet or outside it. Yet once it was plain that neither Heath's policies nor Heath himself could win another General Election, she set about dismantling the barriers to becoming the Tory's first woman leader. By 1979 it was clear that she was an aggressive, tough leader, who was more capable than Heath of inspiring the Tory faithful. The fact that some of her supporters were also frightened by her abrasive and hectoring style did not detract from the success of her campaign, although cartoonists began to express the sharpness of her personality and comments through a sharpness of nose which it is difficult to recognise in photographs.

The most divisive Prime Minister since 1945, Mrs Thatcher presided over a substantial change of ideas about what could be managed in British politics, and what were the sensible goals. As Winston Churchill said about Joseph Chamberlain, she truly "changed the political weather" - to the discomfort of those who suffered under her policies. Although not herself a winner of popularity contests, she won the contests that mattered, and Tory governments were re-elected in 1983 and 1987. Mrs Thatcher was quite prepared to work through agreement, although this usually meant agreeing with her opinions, and President Mitterand of France perhaps captured her best in his observation that "she has the eyes of Caligula but the mouth of Marilyn Monroe."

James Callaghan

One of the generation that served in the Second World War, Jim Callaghan was elected MP for Cardiff South in 1945. Callaghan regretted not having had a university education, and his opponents focussed on this point - Roy Jenkins claiming that he could not recall anyone else who "combines such a powerful political personality with so little intelligence." However, Callaghan's political personality ensured that he not only became Home Secretary and Chancellor of the Exchequer, as Jenkins did, but went on to serve as Foreign Secretary and Prime Minister.

Callaghan was not prominent in the great Labour Party debates of the fifties and sixties, being neither a unilateralist nor a supporter of abandoning Clause Four. In 1963 he was third in the leadership election to succeed Gaitskell, and in the following year Wilson made him Chancellor of the Exchequer. Callaghan had little opportunity of shining in that role, as Labour faced its perennial problems with the economy. It was to his credit that when devaluation became inevitable in 1967, he saw it as equally necessary that he should leave the Treasury and go to the Home Office. There he opposed Barbara Castle's attempt to reform the Trade Unions.

When Labour returned in 1974 Callaghan was made Foreign Secretary and, although he was apparently admired more within the Foreign Office than outside it, he was the preferred successor to Wilson in 1976. Callaghan's immediate concern was somehow to sustain the Labour government in office, which resulted in the agreement with the Liberal Party. However, he also tried to contain the growing left-wing influence within the Labour Party - particularly as represented by Tony Benn - with the result that the left wing criticised him as too conservative, whilst the right wing felt he had not done enough to contain the left. His cosy manner caused him to be dubbed "Uncle Jim", but this did not enable him to survive Thatcher's onslaught.

Denis Healey

Denis Healey became an MP in 1952, and subsequently acquired the reputation - bolstered by his own literary skill - of being the best Prime Minister that Labour never had. An expert in foreign affairs, he was not used in that role by Harold Wilson, but in 1964 was appointed Defence Secretary. When Labour returned precariously to power in 1974 he was made Chancellor of the Exchequer, and Healey's intellectual gifts and debating skills carried him through four years in this office. Like Callaghan, but  unlike Jenkins, Healey was faced with a succession of economic problems whilst Chancellor, and his resolution of these problems led to divisions within the Labour Cabinet. Healey is credited - or discredited - with beginning the monetarist strategy of tightly restricting public spending and limiting pay demands. His obduracy on the latter is widely believed to have exacerbated the strikes in the winter of 1978/1979 – the so-called "Winter of Discontent".

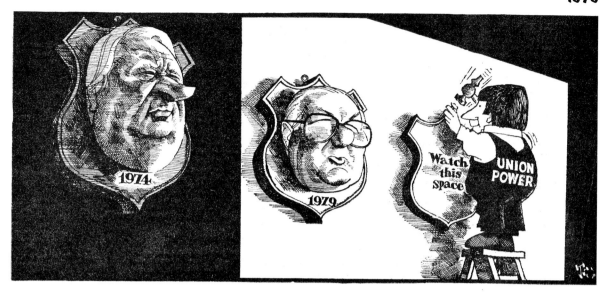

On 6 May 1979 the Observer *carried a cartoon by "Trog" - Wally Fawkes - which posed the question of how Mrs Thatcher would tackle the unions. His cartoon suggests that, having brought down Heath and Callaghan, the unions are already preparing a space on the wall for their next political trophy. In fact it was the unions that became a trophy for Mrs Thatcher.*

Lord Hailsham described Healey as "a piratical old bruiser with a first class mind and very bad manners," and Labour MPs were delighted when he bullied his Conservative opponents - as when he said that being criticised by his Shadow, Geoffrey Howe, was "like being savaged by a dead sheep". However his Labour colleagues were less happy when he applied the same ruthlessness to their own views. After Callaghan's resignation in 1980, many who were in tune with Healey's political stance preferred to vote for Michael Foot as more acceptable to an increasingly left-wing Party. Healey's role in the Labour Party gradually diminished, although cartoonists were naturally reluctant to bid farewell to his bristling eyebrows.

The Result of the 1979 General Election

The turnout of 76.0% was higher than the previous General Election, and the Conservatives were returned with a large majority. Labour received 36.9% of the votes cast, and although this was only 0.2% lower than in February 1974 it was regarded as a major disaster - after all, the 1974 February vote had at least resulted in a Labour government. The result of the 1979 General Election was:

Conservatives	339	43.9%
Labour	267	36.9%
Liberal	11	13.8%
Other	16	5.4%

Significant features of the result were that the Liberals dropped even further back than in October 1974, and there were many fewer Nationalist MPs – four instead of fourteen.

The Cartoonist of the 1979 General Election

Stanley Franklin has been chosen as the cartoonist of the 1979 General Election, not for a single cartoon but for his whole output - particularly his representation of Jim Callaghan as Mr Micawber from Dickens' *David Copperfield*. David Low had used Mr Micawber - always in debt and waiting for something "to turn up" - to parody Churchill, but Franklin used him to catch a particular aspect of Callaghan's personality, and his style of government.

Asked to chose an example of his own work from the 1979 General Election, Franklin says that he would choose one of these Micawber cartoons: "At a Labour Conference someone said to me 'Mr Micawber would like to meet you.' I realised this was an invitation from the Prime Minister. Towering over me, Jim Callaghan said 'So you're the cartoonist who is always attacking me.' I replied 'Mr Callaghan it is the prerogative of the press to attack the Prime Minister.' The Prime Minister said 'Yes I know but *every day*?'".

A Londoner, Franklin's career as political cartoonist started with the *Daily Mirror*, for whom he drew cartoons between 1959 and 1970. From 1974 to 1998 he was political cartoonist for the *Sun* - a frankly tabloid paper with none of the weighty history of the *Daily Mirror*. Given the huge circulations of these papers, Franklin's audience has been larger than that of any cartoonist highlighted in previous Elections, and his influence may have been greater. As Franklin acknowledges, "There can be no doubt that the negative image of a cartoon can do great damage. My depiction of Michael Foot as a dwarf led many people to believe he was a dwarf - politically speaking."

In his cartoons Franklin makes considerable use of a bulbous-nosed figure, known as "Raspberry", who bears a considerable resemblance to W.C. Fields - an actor who famously played Mr Micawber in the 1935 film of *David Copperfield*. The figure of Raspberry appears in his cartoons to ask questions, make statements, or simply to observe the antics of public figures.

Chapter 12
"The Longest Suicide Note in History."

George Gale's cartoon in Tribune *of 13 May 1983 is a cartoon cliché – the start of the Election race. Yet it contains a neat reference to the SDP/Liberal Alliance, with Jenkins and Steel tied together, as their joint leadership was not in fact effective during the election. Margaret Thatcher, of course, holds the starting pistol.*

The Run-up to the 1983 General Election

After her 1979 Election victory, Margaret Thatcher began a period of extraordinary personal and political dominance, despite disputes within her Cabinet and amongst some Conservative backbenchers - who became known as "the wets". Thatcher projected an image of forcing the country to face up to its economic problems, and under her government publicly-owned industries were "privatised", council houses were sold, and Trade Unions were reformed - or disciplined depending on your point of view. Her direct confrontational style of dealing with opponents rested on clear ideological foundations, described as "Thatcherism"; she planned to reduce the size of government, make Britain great again, and encourage people to pay their own way.

Cummings was always keen to portray the ballot box as a trap for the unwary, and his Daily Express *cartoon of 17 May 1983 shows Andropov, the Prime Minister of the Soviet Union, happily receiving the Labour votes. Michael Foot appears with characteristically wild hair, and with a CND emblem over what was in fact his blind eye - a rather offensive touch.*

Thatcher's dominance was made easier by disruption and eventually division within the opposing parties. Their 1979 defeat led to recriminations about how unsocialist the preceding Labour Government had been, to the dominance of left-wing activists in the constituencies, and to fears of their influence in the House of Commons. When Callaghan resigned in October 1980 Michael Foot, the former back bench rebel, was elected as leader of the Labour Party. This was followed in 1981 by the creation of the new Social Democratic Party by right wing Labour Party defectors. In alliance with the Liberal Party the SDP acquired impressive support in the opinion polls, and in some by elections.

The creation of the SDP raised the possibility of "breaking the mould", not only of the two party system, but of the Labour Party itself. Led by the "Gang of Four" -

Roy Jenkins, David Owen, Shirley Williams and Bill Rodgers - the SDP initially attracted "political virgins" who wanted a party that was neither wildly left wing nor radically Conservative, and Labour defectors convinced their own party had become too left wing and anti-Europe. The flow of defectors was increased by Labour left wingers led by Tony Benn, who maintained their angry pursuit of what they proclaimed were Socialist ideals. Wilson and Callaghan had kept the party together in power, but in the bitter context of opposition Michael Foot could hardly be blamed for failing to do so.

The change in the political climate affected the Conservatives as well as Labour, and the position which Mrs Thatcher and her government had reached by 1983 could not have been forecast two years earlier. The opinion polls had shown her to be more unpopular than any post war Prime Minster. This was partly due to the tough monetarist discipline which she

"Trog" - Wally Fawkes - in the Observer of 22 May 1983 shows Thatcher, blind to reality, instructing a nurse to continue the treatment that has turned British industry into a corpse.

Denis Healey - former Defence Secretary and now Shadow Foreign Secretary - joins Foot on the fence in Stanley Franklin's Sun cartoon of 26 May 1983 - although they face in different directions. Labour's manifesto policy was to give up nuclear weapons but to retain Polaris, which Foot said he would not use. The flowers in the "non-nuclear zone" bloom with the CND symbol.

SITTING ON DEFENCE

Superbrats

Peter Brookes' Times *cartoon "Superbrats", of 27 May 1983, refers to the forthcoming Wimbledon championships, and the bad behaviour of the top tennis players. Jim Callaghan has hit his ball directly at Foot, in retaliation for his views on Polaris and Incomes Policy. Meanwhile Jim Prior - one of the Cabinet "wets" - has hit his ball directly at Mrs Thatcher. He had been posted to Northern Ireland but was not happy with the government's economic policy. Roy Jenkins is the ball boy.*

imposed through her Chancellor, Geoffrey Howe, leading to major changes in industry and - eventually - to three million unemployed. However, in retrospect it is clear that the 1982 Falklands War, in which the government successfully mounted a military operation to recapture the Falkland Islands from Argentinean invaders, was the point at which views on Thatcher and the Conservative government changed dramatically.

Election Issues and the 1983 Campaign

Thatcher chose to go the polls a year early, and on 9 May she announced a General Election for 9 June 1983. The polls had provided encouraging news of support for the Conservative government, and had also shown the relative strengths of Thatcher and Foot. Thatcher was certainly not loved by the electorate, but she was admired because she seemed so firmly in charge. In contrast Michael Foot both looked and sounded disorganised, and although he was frequently accompanied by his dog this did not, for once, encourage the British to give him any more support.

The Labour manifesto was published on 16 May 1983 under the title "The New Hope for Britain". It said that a Labour government would leave the EEC, provide a non-nuclear defence, and return privatised industries to public ownership. Its proposals for a massive rise in public spending might have sounded more attractive had they not carried obvious implications for a rise in taxation, and Gerald Kaufman, a member of the Shadow Cabinet, dubbed this manifesto "the longest suicide note in history". By contrast the Conservative manifesto, published two days later, was deliberately unexciting. The focus of the Conservative campaign was to be on Thatcher as an effective leader, by comparison with Michael Foot. Tory newspaper columnists and cartoonists duly emphasised Thatcher's strength as a leader and the unbelievability of Foot as a Prime Minister.

During the Election campaign the SDP/Liberal Alliance did not project itself well, and began to lose its gloss. The split leadership between Roy Jenkins as Prime Minister designate and David Steele as joint leader was confusing, and although Jenkins might look more Prime Ministerial than Foot, he still had no advantage over Margaret Thatcher. Eventually he was pushed to one side. The Labour Party campaign was equally uncertain. The party remained split on defence - specifically over what to do with the remaining nuclear weapon "Polaris". Callaghan and Healey, the Shadow Foreign Secretary, were opposed to the Labour policy of giving it up.

Cummings's Daily Express cartoon [of] May 1983 shows the Labour manifest[o] sinking and the rats departing. Calla[ghan] is already overboard, Healey and Hattersley are preparing to follow, bu[t] Peter Shore looks doubtful. Michael F[oot] has meanwhile lost control and seems destined to go down with the ship, wh[ile] the CND propeller turns in the air. T[he] staring eyes on the funnel indicate th[e] alarming presence of Tony Benn.

Les Gibbard's "Funny way to run a battle" in the Guardian of 27 May 19[83] has Healey and Shore saluting whilst [they] fire off Labour's defence policy - which only succeeds in hitting Foot. Callagh[an,] cutlass between his teeth, manages to board his own ship, whilst on the stric[ken] Tory vessel everyone is surrendering [to] Thatcher, who is making Whitelaw, Py[m] and Prior walk the plank. In the water Jenkins and Steel fire pop-guns from [a] rowing-boat, whilst the Tory publicity advisors Saatchi and Saatchi patrol in [a] submarine.

Funny way to run a battle

Callaghan also raised the spectre of a formal Incomes Policy, and further self-destructiveness occurred over the Falklands War, when Healey made an apparent reference to Margaret Thatcher "glorying in slaughter". The following week Neil Kinnock - now a leading member of the Shadow Cabinet - responded to a comment that Margaret Thatcher had guts by saying it was a pity people had to leave theirs on Goose Green to prove it.

David Steel recalls the 1983 General Election: "The election of 1983 was preceded by the formation of the Liberal-SDP Alliance and a string of by-election victories – Crosby, Croydon, Glasgow-Hillhead, Bermondsey. In our 1981 conference arguing that our success was likely to lead to participation in a coalition government, I concluded my leader's speech with the oft-repeated sentence 'go back to your constituencies and prepare for government'. (At a fringe review a couple of years later this was translated into 'go back to your constituencies and bloody well stay there').

The 1983 campaign was memorable because of the divisions in the Labour Party led by Michael Foot, and the welling-up of support for the sight of two parties, Liberal and SDP, working together. The Falklands factor had restored Conservative fortunes, yet our 'Ask the Alliance' meetings (when genuinely impromptu questions were asked by huge audiences chaired by Ludovic Kennedy, Magnus Magnusson, Steve Race and Bamber Gascoigne) were a great success. So too were our television party political broadcasts featuring me and Roy Jenkins working together, in spite of one unkindly critic likening them to commercials for a gay dating agency.

When Mrs T went off to meet President Reagan at a well-publicised summit, we held a rival one, equally well publicised, at my home in the picturesque village of Ettrick Bridge, which was almost disastrous because fog grounded the helicopters of key participants. Outside our overcrowded eve-of-poll rally in London, I received news of an opinion poll putting us 1% ahead of Labour. I announced this to a cheering crowd from the roof of my battlebus.

On the day we polled 25% - the highest third-force vote recorded at any post-war election - but we only won 23 seats in the 650 House of Commons. Labour with 27% had 209 seats, revealing the fraud of our election system. But from then on we were a credible mass political movement again."

Personalities of the 1983 General Election

Michael Foot

Michael Foot was originally a journalist successful both on Beaverbrook's right-wing *Daily Express* and *Evening Standard* and on the left wing journal *Tribune*. Elected MP in 1945, Foot's first ten years in parliament were full of denunciations of an insufficiently Socialist Labour government and opposition. Foot lost his seat in 1955, but after the death of his hero Nye Bevan in 1960, Foot took his seat in a by-election, and as a leader of the Campaign for Nuclear Disarmament continued to do battle against Gaitskell.

Until Labour's defeat in 1970 Foot continued to be a major left-wing rebel, delivering

" We shall fight in the gutters, we shall fight in the drains . . . !"

his speeches - particularly at Labour Party Conferences - in the angry swoops of a traditional left-wing orator. However, after Labour's defeat he began his progress towards respectability as a potential government minister. This he achieved in February 1974, surprising many people by being relatively effective. In 1980, as a successful left-wing ex-Minister, he was elected as Leader of the Labour Party in succession to Jim Callaghan. He was chosen in preference to Denis Healey, who it was believed would lead from the right and thus cause the break-up of the party. In fact Labour broke up anyway, suggesting that Foot had faced an impossible task.

Foot might have stood a chance against Alec Douglas Home, but not against Margaret Thatcher. His long hair, his pebble glasses, his stick, and his dog were easily caricatured, and critics unfairly focused on his bookish personality and old-fashioned radical style to make him look an unlikely Prime Minister. After Labour's Election defeat in 1983, Foot moved quickly aside to encourage Neil Kinnock's leadership of the Party, and he subsequently behaved impeccably in giving Kinnock loyal support.

Roy Jenkins

Roy Jenkins, who was first elected an MP in 1948, always seemed an unlikely product of a mining background in South Wales. Patrician and Oxford-educated, he showed a centrist and later right-wing revisionist attitude to where the Labour Party should go. A personal and political adherent of Hugh Gaitskell - and no fan of Harold Wilson - Jenkins nevertheless gained office in 1964, and as Home Secretary from 1965 to 1967 he showed himself to be a libertarian, radical reformist. Jenkins talked of the civilised society he hoped to bring about, but critics then and subsequently accused him of creating instead a permissive society - a term of abuse.

In 1967 Jenkins became Chancellor of the Exchequer, and was held to be successful in that role - except by those Labour supporters who blamed him for not introducing a

"We shall fight in the gutters..." by "Jak" - Raymond Jackson - in the Evening Standard *of 2 June 1983 shows Healey emerging from a drain holding a label "Belgrano". The text adapts Churchill's 1940 speech "we shall fight on the beaches, we shall fight on the landing grounds.."*

generous budget before the 1970 General Election. Elected Deputy Leader after the Labour defeat, his career declined as a consequence of his firm adherence to the EEC. Jenkins returned to the Home Office after Labour's 1974 Election victory, but this was in effect a demotion. For personal and political reasons Callaghan refused to give him the Foreign Office in 1976, and this refusal had two consequences: Jenkins went off to be President of the EEC Commission in Brussels, and Callaghan appointed David Owen as Foreign Secretary. Both actions may be seen as leading to the subsequent creation of the Social Democratic Party.

In 1981 Jenkins returned to British politics, and joined Shirley Williams, David Owen and Bill Rodgers to form the SDP. However, he did not return to his previous eminence in the House of Commons, and his obviously growing taste for the good life of food and wine added to a blurring of his political image, and created a target for cartoonists. Jenkins' main political purpose remained the consolidation of Britain's position within the European Community, entry to which he had significantly helped in 1975. He lacked the central egotistical drive necessary to become leader of the Labour Party, or indeed to survive as leader of the SDP/Liberal Alliance, but in different circumstances he would probably have been leader of the Labour Party, rather than Callaghan, Foot or Healey.

David Steel

On his election in 1965 David Steel was the youngest MP. His youthful appearance survived for many years, and he was still being called "the boy David" in the later stages of his political career. Steel originally made his name by pushing through a Private Member's Bill to make abortion more readily available, and in 1975 he succeeded the disgraced Jeremy Thorpe as leader of the Liberal Party. In that role he pressed for a continuing process of coalition , and with Jim Callaghan created the Liberal/Labour Pact which helped to sustain the Labour Government in power for eighteen months.

The 1979 General Election saw a major drop in the Liberal vote, but it also led to the emergence of the Social Democratic Party, which gave Steel the opportunity of creating an Alliance to prevent the two centre parties from fighting each other. This Alliance

On 4 June 1983 Gibbard's Guardian *cartoon "Here's your big chance…" showed Healey's comment as a shot fired through the window of the "Chapel of the Blessed Margaret". As the Tory lynch mob emerges, Healey dashes off an apology and leaves a nervous Michael Foot to convert them to the Labour cause.*

"Here's your big chance — now I've got their attention you convert 'em !"

By the time of Franklin's Sun *cartoon of 31 May 1983 - "I assure you that Roy is still playing a vital role…" - Jenkins had already been sidelined within the SDP/Liberal alliance. Steel addresses the television audience, with David Owen at his side, and Jenkins in the wings making tea. On the same day "Mac" - Stan McMurtry - crossed to the other side of the television screen for his cartoon in the* Daily Mail, *captioned "…And now, a party political broadcast…" Here Steel makes the broadcast while Jenkins does the dusting - his only consolation a bottle of claret among the teacups*

"I ASSURE YOU THAT ROY IS STILL PLAYING A VITAL ROLE IN OUR CAMPAIGN!"

'. . . And now, a party political broadcast on behalf of the SDP-Liberal Alliance . . .'

attracted considerable electoral support, but the "first past the post" system inevitably translated this into a derisory number of seats. Steel also encountered some difficulties in his relationship with Roy Jenkins, who was older and much more experienced, but not hugely energetic. Yet these were insignificant by comparison with the problems he subsequently encountered with David Owen as leader of the SDP.

After the 1987 General Election, Steel headed - perhaps not adroitly - the initiative which led to the merging of the SDP and Liberals into the Liberal Democrats. Critics - especially on the satirical ITV programme "Spitting Image" - portrayed Steel as being in the pocket of the much more dominant David Owen, who opposed the merger.

The Result of the 1983 General Election

The turnout in the 1983 General Election was 72.7% - down from 76% in 1979 - but it was a resounding victory for the Conservatives. They achieved 42.4% of the poll and - through the disproportionate electoral system - gained a huge majority. Paradoxically, in 1964 they had received 43.4% of the poll and lost the election. The results were:

Conservatives	397	42.4%
Labour	209	27.6%
Alliance	23	25.4%
Other	21	4.6%

In the People *of 5 June 1983, "Zoke" - Michael Attwell - used Mrs Thatcher's words against her for his cartoon "Beyond all bounds of public or moral decency..." An ageing Thatcher heartlessly pulls the chain as millions of the unemployed - including teachers and nurses - go down the pan.*

Despite appearances to the contrary, the Alliance actually grew in popularity during the campaign, but this still resulted in a wholly disproportionate acquisition of seats to votes. The Labour Party secured its lowest proportion of the poll since 1918.

"GANGPLANK OF DESPAIR"

3½ MILLION UNEMPLOYED

ZOKE

BEYOND ALL BOUNDS OF PUBLIC OR MORAL DECENCY
MARGARET THATCHER'S WORDS — JUNE 2nd, 1983

Ralph Steadman's cartoon "Foot in the Door", for the New Statesman of 10 June 1983, marked the end of the Election campaign with Margaret Thatcher pirouetting towards No.10 like a figure from the danse macabre. Steadman would later express his disgust at all political cartooning, asserting that "most cartoonists are toadies playing the game politicians want them to play."

Cartoonist of the 1983 General Election

Jak has been chosen as cartoonist of the 1983 General Election, largely for his cartoon "We shall fight in the gutters..." in the *Evening Standard* of 2 June 1983. In an intemperate moment Denis Healey had referred to Mrs Thatcher's "glorying in slaughter" after the sinking of the Argentinean warship General Belgrano the previous year, and Jak used two historic references to produce his striking cartoon. The caption refers to Churchill's wartime exhortation that the British should "fight on the beaches...", whilst the image itself refers to the famous 1954 *Washington Post* cartoon by "Herblock" - Herbert Block - showing Richard Nixon climbing out of a sewer.

"Jak" - Raymond Jackson - joined the *Evening Standard* in 1952, as illustrator on the television page, but after Vicky's death in 1966 he took over his role as political cartoonist. On the whole Jak's cartoons were intended to make people laugh, and he was less dominated by the need to draw political cartoons than Low or Vicky, his predecessors on the paper. His heavy workload also included drawing for the *Daily Express*, *Daily Mail* and *Mail on Sunday*, and he followed Strube in publishing an annual collection of his cartoons.

On the front cover of one posthumous collection of his works Jak was described as "Britain's best loved cartoonist" - not an attribution likely to be given to Low or Vicky. Unlike them he did not produce a cartoon which encapsulated a political personality, and became part of political history, but he was good at presenting an easily recognisable idea. In his thirty years as political cartoonist with the *Evening Standard* he was as capable than any other cartoonist of arousing deep passions amongst those he criticised, especially trade unions and the Irish.

HAVING LISTENED TO THE RADIO NEWS ON HIS JOURNEY IN —— HE SKIMS THE DAY'S NEWSPAPERS AND SETS TO WORK WITH A 2B PENCIL, AN A2 LAYOUT PAD AND A MUG OF HOT COFFEE...

Chapter 13
Thatcher Moves Forward.

During the 1987 Election campaign the opinion polls consistently showed Labour well behind the Conservatives. In his London Daily News cartoon of 18 May 1987, "Trog" - Wally Fawkes - shows Dennis Thatcher, the Prime Minister's husband, being disciplined for raising even a suspicion of failure. Dennis was supposed to refer to his wife as "the boss".

The Run-up to the 1987 General Election

The Conservative party's 1983 Election victory ushered in a second stage of Thatcherism, in which the most fundamental feature was the return of companies and industries from public to private ownership. The most significant results of this process were an extension of share ownership - to include a wider proportion of the population - and a sudden capital gain for the government. This permitted Nigel Lawson, as Chancellor of the Exchequer, to reduce income tax in successive budgets - although it was noticeable that the revenue from other taxes went up.

The rhetoric of Thatcherism emphasised self-help accompanied by direct State intervention on education, health and local government. As a result of continued high unemployment, and the application of more restrictive Trade Union laws, the Conservative government had to deal with many fewer strikes. The major exception was a strike in the mining industry which began in March 1984 and lasted for a year, but this ended in defeat for the National Union of Mineworkers. During this strike the Labour leadership just managed the delicate balancing act of not supporting the miners, and yet not condemning the strike.

The problems of Northern Ireland persisted, and in October 1984 erupted in a most dramatic form with an attempt to kill Margaret Thatcher and other Cabinet Ministers in the Grand Hotel at Brighton. Overseas Mrs Thatcher maintained a wary and perhaps even antagonistic relationship

mac

"Would you tell Glenys I've announced the manifesto and if she's got a minute I'd like to know what to do next . . ."

with fellow members of the EEC. However, her signing of the Single European Act of 1986 gave more central authority to the EEC, and became a major issue for intra-party conflict.

Michael Foot had resigned immediately after Labour's 1983 Election defeat, and he was followed as leader of the Labour Party by Neil Kinnock - a left-winger and supporter of the Campaign for Nuclear Disarmament. Kinnock had no experience in government, but as party leader he worked to move the Labour Party away from the commitments in its 1983 "suicide note", and to expel Militant - an extreme left-wing sect within the party. The

The Daily Mail of 20 May 1987 carried a cartoon by "Mac" - Stan McMurtry - suggesting that the relationship between Neil Kinnock and his wife Glenys was quite different to that of the Thatchers. Glenys is shown as the unofficial "Minister for Women", who is too busy to give her husband advice on the Election campaign.

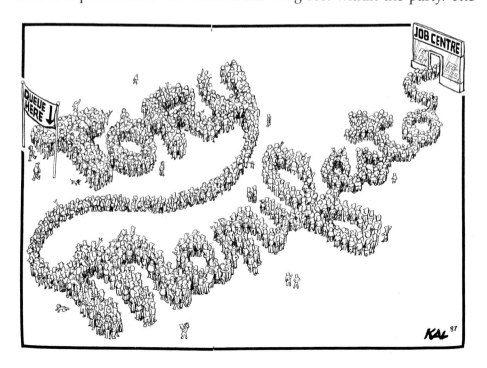

In Today of 20 May 1987 the American cartoonist "Kal" - Kevin Kallaugher - referred back to the 1979 General Election campaign, where one Conservatives poster had shown an unemployment queue to prove the point that "Labour isn't working". Unemployment figures were still high in 1987, and Kal neatly reversed the Conservative image.

POWER TO THE PEOPLE? I MEANT, OF COURSE, POWER TO THE PERSON!

PRIME MINISTER FOR LIFE

THE NEXT MOVES FORWARD ON & ON & ON & ON & ON & ON

Martin Rowson's cartoon "Power to the people?...", in Today *of 21 May 1987, picked up Margaret Thatcher's comment that she would go on and on and on as Prime Minister. The sinister figure holding her laurel-wreath is Normal Tebbit, whilst the bearers of her imperial cloak are Douglas Hurd, Geoffrey Howe, a decaying Willie Whitelaw, and Nigel Lawson.*

SDP and Liberals continued in coalition as the Alliance, but David Owen pushed out Roy Jenkins and formed a dual leadership with David Steel. Owen was against merging the two parties, but wanted to continue the electoral pact, for this was the focus of the Alliance and sustained its supporters through occasional by-election victories.

Election Issues and the 1987 Campaign

On 11 May the General Election was announced for 11 June 1987. The campaign revolved around a Conservative government which could claim considerable economic success, and which identified itself with a visibly-strong leader. Characteristically, Margaret Thatcher was accompanied by her ministers at Election press conferences, but answered nearly all the questions herself. She was not well liked by the electorate, but she was respected. By comparison Neil Kinnock was often portrayed as a lightweight, who still had to overcome some aspects of his left-wing past, whilst the Alliance suffered from two leaders who not only differed in style and personality, but occasionally also on policy.

The Conservative manifesto "The Next Moves Forward" was a promise to continue what was already underway, plus a new community charge which was not seen as creating any major problems. When Labour published its own manifesto Mrs Thatcher used the sort of imagery loved by Tory cartoonists, and described it as an iceberg with socialist dangers under the surface. It talked about a wealth tax, about returning British Gas and British Telecommunications to "social ownership", and about job creation schemes - but not withdrawal from the EEC.

The problem for Labour was that Kinnock's remedial work had not extended so far as to create enthusiasm among disaffected Labour voters.

In the Daily Express *of 22 May, and again in the* Sunday Express *of 24 May 1987, Cummings tried a fishy metaphor for his constant theme of a Labour Party dominated by the hard left. In both images Neil Kinnock is dominated by the more ferocious figure of Ken Livingstone, famous former leader of the Greater London Council. Livingstone's interest in newts was one of the few humanising characteristics which cartoonists ever allowed to a left-wing politician.*

"The Alliance plans to unify the Nation, not with three parties, but now FOUR!"

For the Daily Express *of 5 June 1987 Cummings used the cartoonist's favourite image of a coalition as an ass with two heads. In "'The Alliance plans to unify the Nation…'" Owen and Steel are shown as splitting apart through their undoubted differences on defence, and Cummings helpfully provided numbers in case any reader failed to count the four politicians.*

The party might present itself not only as the initiator of the popular National Health Service, but also as the best defender of it, but this was one of the few areas in which people accepted that a Labour government might be more effective than a Tory one. The high number of unemployed might have worked in Labour's favour, for it remained despite the government's massaging of the figures. Unfortunately much unemployment was regional, and was regarded by the even larger number of the employed as a price worth paying - particularly as someone else was paying it.

In a campaign without other major issues, intentions in relation to the National Health Service made headlines. Mrs Thatcher defiantly proclaimed the virtues of using private healthcare, while the revelations that Denis Healey's wife had gone to a private hospital for a hip operation was also seized on by the media. As in the 1983 General Election campaign, defence emerged as an Election issue, highlighting differences not only between the parties but also within the Labour Party. Kinnock's uncertainty over the role of nuclear weapons was mocked as a "hands up" response to Russian aggression, and the Conservatives also attacked his social programme, claiming that huge tax increases would be necessary to pay for Labour's promises.

Kinnock actually received the plaudits of the media for running an effective Election campaign, and in particular for a party political broadcast that focused on him as a caring, family man. The problem was that Kinnock still seemed unable to persuade the new share owners in former council houses to return to voting Labour.

Norman Tebbit, Chairman of the Conservative Party in 1987, remembers the General Election:

"The Election of 1987 was won at the Conservative Party Conference in 1986. There, under the slogan 'The Next Moves Forward', platform speeches focused on the Thatcher Government's continuing programme of reforms. Ministerial speeches all listed four key 'moves forward' to be made over the ensuing years. As each speech ended the posters listing those moves went up throughout the Conference Centre. The polls moved decisively in favour of the Government.

The campaign itself went as planned. Awkward issues were raised early in the campaign and covered to the onset of electoral boredom. It finished strongly focused on the economy. Our polling had shown that voters believed they were over-taxed, and got poorer value for money, when local authorities or government spent their money than they did when they spent it themselves - and our campaign played to that belief. The Alliance challenge was undermined by showing that it was split on many issues between its SDP and its Liberal components. Had it presented a stronger challenge, Plan B was ready - to switch our fire from Labour to the Alliance.

The Government started as clear favourites - only a terrible error on our part could have lost the election, so a 'safety first' campaign was needed. The media folk and pundits declared that we fought a dull campaign. Labour's, it was said, was better, but Labour's 'brilliant' display cut no ice with the voters."

The News on Sunday *of 7 June 1987 carried Ralph Steadman's drawing "Into the Blue!", dealing with the north-south divide - a feature of contemporary politics rarely emphasised in cartoons. The north had suffered disproportionately from economic changes due to its dependence on traditional manufacturing industry, and Mrs Thatcher is happy to launch it towards the Arctic.*

HIPPOCRATIC OATH   HYPOCRITIC OATH

The National Health Service was a battleground for the major parties, with Labour constantly accusing the Conservatives of undermining it through private healthcare. Mrs Thatcher memorably stated that the NHS was "safe in my hands", but Gibbard's cartoon "Hippocratic Oath - Hippocritic Oath", from the Guardian *of 5 June 1987, shows her preparing to enter a private hospital, while tired doctors walk through a crowded NHS waiting-room.*

Personalities of the 1987 General Election

Neil Kinnock

Neil Kinnock was first elected an MP in 1970, and achieved initial prominence as a left-winger, campaigning against membership of the EEC and against the Labour Government's cuts in 1976. A supporter of CND, Kinnock's views had a lot in common with those of his colleague Tony Benn, but in 1980 he signalled his distance from Benn by not supporting him in the election for deputy leader. Reactions to this showed that there is no fury like the left-wing of the Labour Party accusing its colleagues of "betraying Socialism" - unless it is the right wing of the Conservative Party accusing others of "betraying Thatcherism".

Kinnock became leader of the Labour Party in 1983, on the resignation of Michael Foot, and in the succeeding four years he established himself in a strong position by holding his party together, with no more departures from left or right. A striking public speaker, who could touch heights of eloquence matched only by Michael Heseltine on the Conservative side, his denunciation of the Militant sect at the Labour Conference in 1985 confirmed his oratorical powers. Kinnock started the process of revising Labour's policies which was later brought to fruition by Tony Blair, but in an age increasingly dominated by television, the oratory that could stimulate and excite the faithful often appeared uncomfortably dramatic. By the 1987 Election Kinnock was already being referred to as the "Welsh windbag".

Kinnock proved less than effective in combating Margaret Thatcher in the House of Commons, and outside Parliament he and his wife Glenys were targeted by the largely Conservative press. The newspaper reports and articles provided material from which cartoonists worked, and Kinnock found himself pilloried in dozens of unflattering cartoons.

David Owen

David Owen - a medical doctor - was elected to the Commons in 1966 as a Labour MP, and became a Naval Minister in 1968. In 1972 he was one of the sixty-nine Labour MPs who voted in favour of joining the Common Market, although this was not held against him, and in 1974, when Wilson returned to power, he became a Health Minister.

In 1977, on the death of Anthony Crosland, Jim Callaghan made Owen Foreign Secretary, in a move reminiscent of the appointment of an equally-youthful Anthony Eden to the same post before the war. Yet after Labour's 1979 Election defeat Owen became disenchanted with the general leftward shift of the party, with its movement

On 7 June 1987 Trog's cartoon in the Observer showed another favourite image of political cartoonists faced with coalition - Owen and Steel are running three-legged in the Election race, and are only left with the dust of the other candidates.

away from Europe, and with the new process for electing the leader. As a result in 1980 he joined Shirley Williams, Bill Rodgers and - more reluctantly - Roy Jenkins to form the Social Democratic Party.

Owen's wish to get away from what he called the "fudge and mudge" of the Labour Party suggested that he had clear views about issues, but this breach seemed increasingly a matter of self belief rather than of policies. Owen admired Margaret Thatcher, perhaps because - like her - he was more interested in whether people respected him than whether they liked him. In fact dislike was a common phenomenon among those around him.

By the time of the 1987 General Election, Owen was joint leader of the Alliance with David Steel, but his more assertive personality, and willingness to engage in sharp public debate, memorably resulted in the Spitting Image puppeteers portraying him as having Steel in his pocket. However, Owen proved to be wholly opposed to merging with the Liberals, lost the vote in the SDP on this issue, and in consequence largely disappeared from politics.

On Election Day - 11 June 1987 - Nicholas Garland's Daily Telegraph cartoon showed Owen and Steel as tortoises ill-equipped for catching either Kinnock or Thatcher, who race for the finishing line as hares.

"Naturally I can scrap immigration controls—because when I get to power, no one in their right mind will want to come to Britain!"

Cummings' cartoon "'Naturally I can scrap immigration controls…'", from the Sunday Express *of 7 June 1987, draws attention to immigration - although this was not an issue in the Election campaign. Kinnock stands in the south of England, but the monsters of the left have their feet in the north - Arthur Scargill, the miners' leader, Ken Livingstone, and Roy Hattersley, the Shadow Chancellor. Kinnock had stepped away from unilateral disarmament, but his union flag still contains the CND symbol.*

The Result of the 1987 General Election

As expected, the Conservatives returned with a huge majority, on a turnout of 75.3%. Labour secured only 30.8% of the poll - their second lowest in sixty years - but they achieved their main objective by preventing the Alliance from taking over as the second party. The final results were:

Conservatives	376	42.2%
Labour	229	30.8%
Alliance	22	22.6%
Others	23	4.3%

The Cartoonist of the 1987 General Election

"Trog" - Wally Fawkes - has been chosen as the cartoonist of the 1987 General Election, largely for his cartoon of Dennis Thatcher in the short-lived London *Daily News* of 18 May 1987. The appearance of wives or husbands of Prime Ministers in General Election cartoons is a relatively recent phenomenon, and seems to have begun with Mary Wilson in 1970. Only Trog has so far made the Prime Minister's spouse the sole feature of a political cartoon.

Wally Fawkes acquired his nickname by performing as a clarinettist in a jazz band called "the Troglodytes". Another expatriate cartoonist - born in Vancouver, Canada - Fawkes came to Britain as a schoolboy, and has appeared in perhaps the widest range of newspapers and periodicals of any contemporary cartoonist. He was introduced to the *Daily Mail* by Leslie Illingworth, and did some of his best early work there, being their main cartoonist from 1968 to 1971. However, from 1965 to 1996 his main work appeared in the *Observer*, but he also drew for *Punch* - especially front covers, and like Nicholas Garland he drew for both the *Spectator* and the *New Statesman*.

Whatever the journal, Fawkes' style has remained remarkably consistent over forty years. His figures tend to be large and clear, and unlike some contemporary cartoonists he seems able to make the reader both laugh and wince. Outside the election sphere he has some claim to be the first major cartoonist to publish a caricature of Queen Elizabeth II.

By the time that Les Gibbard's cartoon appeared in the Guardian *of 12 June 1987, the result of the General Election was already known. As he shows, Kinnock and Hattersley might have crossed swords with Steel and Owen, but they were still no more than a guard of honour for the electoral wedding of Margaret Thatcher and a rather startled John Bull. The expressions of her opponents neatly capture the dismay that contributed to the creation of New Labour.*

126

Chapter 14
Triumph of the Soapbox?

Cummings was always looking for ways to illustrate his conviction that the Labour Party was secretly dominated by the hard left. His Sunday Express cartoon of 15 March 1992 shows Kinnock as hollow and directionless, his movements controlled by an army of fanatical left wingers hidden from the electorate. A wild-eyed Tony Benn makes his obligatory appearance.

"The moment he gets into Downing St, we make him take off the double-breasted suit and put on Tshirt, jeans & trainers"

The BUDGETs that could not BUDGE IT.——— or ———A Congeſtion in ye BODY POLITICK !!!

The Run up to the 1992 General Election

After her 1987 Election victory, Margaret Thatcher's Conservative government continued - unsurprisingly - with the policies she believed were transforming Britain. The major initiatives of privatisation, of council house sales, and of the constraint of trade unions through employment law seemed to provide an effective basis for continued success.

As Chancellor of the Exchequer, Nigel Lawson managed to achieve an early economic boom - although this was followed by a predictable slump. He also put his faith in lower taxes on higher incomes, hoping it would lead to managerial initiatives and improved economic performance, but the result was inconclusive. The government's "reforms" in the educational system, and the introduction of "internal markets" in the National Health Service, proved to be unpopular, but were not as controversial as the government's new method of paying for local government which it called the "Community Charge" - quickly dubbed the Poll Tax. This was seen as unfair and proved deeply unpopular - on 31 March 1990 a massive and

Martin Rowson's cartoon in the Independent *of 25 March 1992 imagined "What if...Gillray were alive…", and employed the scatological style of the great eighteenth-century cartoonist James Gillray. In an image full of incident, John Smith, Shadow Chancellor of the Exchequer, administers "Syrup of Figures" to Kinnock, while Norman Lamont gives "Tax Cut Laxative" to John Major, with appropriate results. Chris Patten, Chairman of the Conservative Party, stands ready with a chamber pot, as Ashdown protests.*

27.3

"BRING OUT YOUR DEAD."

Nicholas Garland's cartoon "Bring Out Your Dead", from the Daily Telegraph *of 27 March 1992, comments on the efforts by Robin Cook, Shadow Health Spokesman, in turning the decline of the National Health Service to Labour's advantage.*

partially-violent demonstration against it on the streets of London proved a major disturbance to British political life.

Once again the issues most hotly debated by politicians were dwarfed by external events which seemed to have little impact on voters. The disintegration of the Soviet Empire, the release of Nelson Mandela, and continued death and violence in and about Northern Ireland were not matters of dispute between the political parties. Yet Margaret Thatcher's belligerent attitude to Britain's European partners did become a defining feature of her leadership. It is unlikely that the vast majority of British electors were terribly disturbed at the sight of Mrs Thatcher shouting at foreigners, for although the Labour Party moved itself towards a more

In the Sunday Telegraph *on 29 March 1992, Willie Rushton presented the Election campaign as a version of the popular television programme "Blind Date", in which a woman has to choose a partner for a date without ever seeing the candidates. Cilla Black stands behind the screen with an unusually elderly Britannia, who is about to choose between Major, Kinnock, and Ashdown.*

Blind Date

Chris Riddell's cartoon in the Independent *of 29 March 1992 refers to Edvard Munch's 1893 painting "The Scream". The small figure is Jennifer Bennett, whose wait for an NHS ear operation had featured in a controversial Labour Party Political Broadcast the previous week. The facts were challenged, and the* Sun *demanded to know "If Kinnock will tell lies about a sick little girl, will he ever tell the truth about anything?"*

positive engagement with Europe, it apparently received no significant public-opinion advantage from doing so. However, in October 1990 it was Mrs Thatcher's emphatic "No! No! No!" to closer European integration, delivered in the House of Commons during Prime Minister's Questions, which led to the resignation of Geoffrey Howe, and to her eventual resignation as Prime Minister.

In Howe's resignation speech of November 1990 he cut his leader's throat with an air of sad regret, creating a House of Commons sensation that precipitated Thatcher's departure. Her chosen successor was not the eloquent and charismatic Michael Heseltine, but John Major, who became Conservative leader and Prime Minister at the end of the month. Major's colleagues, the media, and the electorate seemed to prefer his relatively low-key listening style, and he acquired a higher standing in the opinion polls than either Thatcher or Kinnock. Heseltine, who became a senior minister again, proved to be a very effective loyal helper.

While the government was preoccupied by internal debates, the Labour Party was struggling to reinvent itself. It transformed itself into a party that favoured closer integration with Europe - especially through the Social Chapter which could be helpful to many of its core supporters. Labour

Steve Bell's cartoon "No way are we fighting a negative campaign…", in the Guardian *of 31 March 1992, shows the Conservatives' fervent denial that their campaign is based on criticising Labour. Major, Patten, Lamont, and Heseltine shake their heads vigorously, but the poster behind Heseltine carries an image from the "Labour's Tax Bombshell" campaign, launched two months earlier.*

also attempted to demonstrate that its policies were realistic, calculating how the increased social policies and the attempt to reduce unemployment could be paid for without increasing taxes for the majority of the population. Kinnock and his colleagues worked on the premise that the electorate wanted sound economic policies, not just good social services.

The Alliance - which in 1987 had fallen back from its 1983 peak - continued to have problems. The vast majority of the Liberal Party, and a significant majority of the Social Democrats, wanted a merger between the parties, but David Owen did not and when he lost the vote he largely disappeared from politics. In July 1988 David Steel was succeeded as Leader of the newly-titled Liberal Democrats by Paddy Ashdown, who offered the vigorous style to be expected of a former army officer. Politically he advocated equal distance from both Labour and Conservatives, whilst David Owen reached the end of his political journey by advising people to vote Conservative rather than Liberal Democrat. Many Labour supporters rejoiced at this confirmation of what they had always believed about him.

On 6 April 1992 Charles Griffin's Daily Mirror *cartoon used that old favourite of cartoonists - the Election as a horse race. Kinnock goes into the lead, while Major bounces along on his soapbox strapped to Chris Patten, the Chairman of the Conservative Party. Ashdown trails far behind, and Margaret Thatcher's strange position reflects her comment that when she left office she would be a driver from the back seat.*

As the election neared, party publicity machines ran at full throttle . . .

'. . . There's this real scary scene involving a huge and hideous budget deficit'

Election Issues and the 1992 General Election Campaign

Major held on for as long as he could, hoping for improvements in the economy and therefore in the public opinion polls. Unfortunately neither of these had occurred by 11 March, when he announced the General Election for 9 April 1992.

The election coincided with a Budget, in which Norman Lamont provided some anticipated benefits for the taxpayer. A week later, Labour's Shadow Chancellor, John Smith, produced an alternative in which he attempted to show how tax and spending could be reconciled. He proposed to achieve this by increasing taxes on the wealthy, claiming that eight out of ten electors would be better off. Subsequent events did not demonstrate the supposed willingness of people to pay more tax to support better services. An example of what the management theorist Chris Argyris calls Espoused Theory versus Theory in use.

Labour produced what many regarded as its most "responsible" manifesto for many years. It offered support for Europe, increased expenditure on education and training, action on unemployment and increased spending on the National Health Service. The longstanding problem over Labour's attitude to defence was resolved by acknowledging the need for nuclear weapons, whilst it was accepted that most trade union constraints would be retained and there would be no renationalisation. Defence and nationalisation were not major campaigning issues, for the first time in several General Elections.

In fact, the most significant issues within the General Election campaign were not only regarded as pretty trivial at the time, but have come to seem even more so in retrospect. On 24 March 1992, for example, the Labour Party produced a television Party Political Broadcast emphasising the ease with which one young girl got an ear operation through private health, whilst

Dave Gaskill's cartoon from Today *on 1 April 1992, dutifully repeats John Major's warning of "Nightmare on Kinnock Street" from the previous day, with a film poster based on the "Nightmare on Elm Street" series of horror films. Kinnock appears as Freddy Krueger, Lamont as Dracula, and Major as Frankenstein's monster. On 8 April 1992, the day before polling, the* Sun *ran eight pages of text attacking Labour, under the banner headline "Nightmare on Kinnock Street".*

another - later identified as Jennifer Bennett - was forced to wait for treatment under the National Health Service. The "War of Jennifer's Ear" blew up when her grandfather, a staunch Conservative, disputed the facts and tipped off Conservative Central Office, who in turn fed the story to the *Daily Express*.

Labour's new line of responsible and moderate government was directly opposed by a Conservative poster campaign that declared "You can't trust Labour", and introduced the Labour "Double Whammy" of taxes and prices - an obscure reference explained by a picture of a boxer with "1. More Taxes" and "2. Higher Prices" written on his gloves. The opinion polls suggested that electors were indeed attracted to the apparently decent, relatively moderate John Major, rather than to Neil Kinnock. Major himself attributed a considerable part of his success to his ability to "connect" with the public, and emphasised this by standing on a soapbox to address the crowds - an image seized on by several cartoonists. He also courted popularity in England by his passionate advocacy of the integrity of the United Kingdom - meaning no devolution for Scotland or Wales.

Stanley Franklin's cartoon "I've fitted a door flap…" in the Sun *on 4 April 1992 shows Kinnock as the unions' poodle - a point of view that was really untenable by this date, but was presumably calculated to find echoes in the minds of* Sun *readers.*

Another significant event in the Election campaign was a Labour rally at Sheffield on 1 April 1992, a week before the poll. This rally had been planned for eighteen months, and seemed to have gone very well, but it quickly came to be regarded as a piece of "triumphalism", apparently demonstrating that Labour and especially Neil Kinnock were overconfident of victory. This impression was reinforced by the brief clips of the event shown on television, making an interesting contrast between the event

"I'VE FITTED A DOOR FLAP IN CASE KINNOCK BECOMES PREMIER!"

In the Sunday Telegraph *of 5 April 1992 Willie Rushton picked up John Major's attack on the Liberal Democrats as Labour's "Trojan Horse", showing him as a wild-haired soothsayer delivering the warning from his famous soapbox. Paddy Ashdown sits triumphantly astride the wooden horse outside the walls of No.10, while inside lurk Kinnock and Labour's Deputy Leader, Roy Hattersley.*

itself and the media coverage. Support for Labour dropped over the weekend, and the Sheffield rally may well have contributed to the Conservative success, although it is difficult to find direct links between an Election result and the preceding campaign, let alone any particular event within it.

In common with most of the tabloid newspapers, the *Sun* showed itself violently anti-Labour, and especially anti-Kinnock, during the Election campaign. On polling day its front page showed Neil Kinnock's head inside a light bulb with the headline "If Kinnock Wins Today Will the Last Person in Britain Please Turn Out the Lights". As immodest in its pride as in its use of page-three women, the paper subsequently celebrated the Election results with the headline "It's the Sun wot won it". This claim partly rested on the paper's enormous national circulation - 22% of the adult population - and partly on the fact that its readers were less politically-interested than many others. The impact of the paper's opposition is impossible to measure, but many Labour supporters saw it as part of a wider negative campaign.

In Luton on 28 March 1992 John Major tried to get closer to the voters by standing on a soapbox and speaking through a hand-held megaphone. In the Independent *on 6 April 1992, Riddell extended the soapbox image to Major's whole campaign, showing him being marketed like a soap powder, with "that bluey greyness you can trust" - the Conservative colour being blue and Major being often portrayed as grey. Unfortunately the electorate seems to have no brand loyalty.*

John Major writes of the 1992 Election: "When I became Prime Minister in November 1990 I knew an election could not be long delayed and yet nor could it be imminent. The Conservative Party was split. We had been far behind in the opinion polls for months. European policy was a divisive running sore. The Poll Tax had led to riots in the streets. And the economy was heading for a deep recession. Interest Rates were at 14%, inflation was nearly in double figures and unemployment was rising rapidly and, in due course, would nearly reach 3 million. It was an unpromising inheritance.

And yet I believed we could win. This belief was a mixture of calculation and intuition: I did not believe fate had carried me from Brixton to Downing Street as only a short-term tenant.

I delayed the Election date for fifteen months and finally called it for 9 April 1992 – the twenty-second anniversary of the day Norma and I had met. It would, I hoped, be a good omen.

The campaign did not begin well. The media anticipated a Labour victory and so did some of the Conservative old guard. When I raised the perils of devolution to the United Kingdom I was outraged to learn that officials at Central Office told the media to ignore them and concentrate on the economy.

An early idea to hold meetings open to any member of the public flopped. The police feared I might be shot. Central Office had a worse nightmare: that disruption of these meetings would produce bad television pictures. The meetings became all-ticket and lost their purpose as the press refused to believe the questions were spontaneous.

On the streets of Bolton I faced a riot and – for security reasons – was bundled into the 'Battlebus' and driven off. I was determined not to let this occur again and decided to carry an old fashioned soapbox with me from which I intended to confront any future demonstration. The soapbox made its debut in Luton and became a feature of the campaign.

On Election Day the result looked like a dead heat and even as the polls closed I learned of an Exit Poll predicting a hung Parliament. It was not to be. We won, but with only a tiny and uncertain majority despite a big lead in votes cast. That small majority was to prove our undoing and a later Election was to have a less happy result.

But, in 1992, the electoral cycle was defeated: we had won an election that should have been lost."

Personality of the 1992 General Election

John Major

John Major was a Londoner, and was a Borough Councillor before his election as MP for a country seat, Huntingdonshire, in 1979. The son of an elderly father who was famously both a circus performer and a producer of garden gnomes, Major, like Margaret Thatcher, had supposedly "classless" origins. A hard worker with a capacity to grasp detail, Major first came to prominence in 1987 as Chief Secretary at the Treasury. When Thatcher promoted him to the Foreign Office in 1989 it was to the surprise of many - including himself - as he had previously shown no great interest in foreign affairs. More sensibly she moved him to the Treasury on the resignation of Nigel Lawson later in 1989.

By the time of the 1992 General Election John Major still had the advantages of being a fresh and obviously-pleasant Prime Minister. Two years earlier he had been the last of several people who attracted Margaret Thatcher's attention as potential successors to herself. When the succession became more imminent, Major acquired the support both of relatively uncommitted Tory MPs - who saw him as an attractive alternative to Thatcher, and of the committed Thatcherites - who abandoned the regicide Michael Heseltine in favour of a man they believed him to be "one of us". As his colleague Kenneth Clarke put it, Major would deliver "Thatcherism with a human face". Major was certainly more open than Thatcher, starting his first Cabinet as Prime Minister with the exclamation "Well, who would have thought it".

During the 1992 General Election campaign Major adopted the soapbox as a distinguishing feature of his populist approach. This image of accessibility and confidence had explicit reference to a more pleasant era of British politics and social life, which was also invoked by his speeches. Major's 1992 Election victory surprised many people, but not himself. However, his next five years as Prime Minister were to see him slipping downhill, and cartoonists increasingly portrayed him as dull and grey - until Steve Bell finally skewered him.

The Observer's *cartoon of 12 April 1992 by "Trog" - Wally Fawkes - captures the disappointment felt by Labour voters in the General Election result. The slogan "It's time for Labour" was taken from the Labour Party manifesto, but the champagne "opened in error" and the scrapped Queen's speech - announcing new legislation - carry echoes of the ill-fated Sheffield rally.*

The Result of the 1992 General Election

The 1992 General Election saw the Conservatives achieve 14.1 million votes - their largest total ever. The revised Labour Party could not persuade the electorate that it had genuinely changed, and despite the predictions of a hung parliament the Conservatives secured an overall majority of 21 seats. The results were:

Conservatives	336	41.9%
Labour	271	34.4%
Liberal Democrats	20	17.9%
Other	24	5.8%

The Cartoonist of the 1992 General Election

Willie Rushton was a founder-member of the satirical magazine *Private Eye* in 1961, and was known as the contributor of small cartoons to that magazine, as well as for his appearances on the satirical television show "That Was the Week that Was", and as a writer and radio broadcaster. His *Private Eye* cartoons became a characteristic feature of the magazine - particularly the "Little Gnittie" masthead, a parody of the crusader logo on the *Daily Express*.

Before the foundation of *Private Eye* Rushton had worked as political cartoonist for the *Liberal News*, but the 1992 General Election was the only one in which his newspaper cartoons were a prominent feature, for he was employed by the *Sunday Telegraph*. Rushton has been chosen as the cartoonist of that campaign for the range and idiosyncratic brilliance of his cartoons. As the two examples included here demonstrate, he was equally at home working with classical allusions as with references to popular television shows.

Chapter 15
Teeth and Sleaze.

The Run-up to the 1997 General Election

Cartoonists have frequently used the image of a starting pistol to begin the Election, but Dave Brown's cartoon in the Independent *of 18 March 1997 provided the less hackneyed metaphor of a rocket. John Major is portrayed as a flightless Dodo, committing itself to extinction by asking the Queen to light the fuse that will launch the General Election. Brown had first drawn Major as a Dodo three months earlier, recalling that the image "seemed to perfectly suit Major, both as a signifier that he was inexorably heading for extinction, and on the physical level of his awkward looks and manner."*

The Conservatives found that the euphoria of their 1992 General Election victory dissipated rather quickly. A series of events led to a total collapse in the credibility of John Major's government for dealing with economic matters - always previously a crucial Conservative asset, and on 16 September 1992 - "Black Wednesday" - Major and his Chancellor Norman Lamont found themselves fighting desperately to keep Britain within the European Exchange Rate Mechanism. The subsequent gradual recovery in the economy was neither sufficiently clear, nor sufficiently attributable to good government for this to benefit the Conservative Party in the 1997 Election campaign.

Queen Mary - Henry VIII's daughter - said that when she was dead and opened they would find "Calais" lying in her heart, but John Major would have at least two words lying on his - "Europe" and "Sleaze". The first became a perennial problem, and the level of willing participation in the development of the European Union was a constant source of division within the Conservative Party. Labour was able to avoid such open conflicts, but Major was faced with votes against him by Tory rebels, and with divisions in his own Cabinet. His unintentionally-public comment about the "four bastards" in his Cabinet was perhaps unduly selective. Major eventually adopted a policy of "wait and see" on Europe - using a strategy first adopted by Prime Minister Asquith in relation to Ulster nearly ninety years earlier.

"Sleaze" provided another set of problems for John Major. The public could be forgiven for not understanding the nuances of European policy, but they had a clear grasp of the money and sex scandals involving both

Conservative ministers and back-benchers. In October 1993 Major had launched a strategy of "Back to Basics", by which he meant higher school standards, better law and order, and commonsense economics. However, this slogan was subsequently adopted as a rallying-cry for the "moral majority" in his party, eager to impose their ideas of appropriate sexual behaviour, and was then used by the media as a licence for exposing sexual scandals. The acceptance of payment for parliamentary favours was also something the general public could understand and dislike, even if they did not always understand the arcane rules that were being broken.

By polling day in 1997 Labour had been out of office for eighteen years. Neil Kinnock had resigned four days after Labour's 1992 General Election defeat, and was succeeded by John Smith, who further advanced the

Nicholas Garland's cartoon in the Daily Telegraph *of 20 March 1997 shows the crowd sleeping through a gladiatorial contest between Blair, Ashdown, and Major. Garland's intuition would seem to have been correct, as the turnout in the 1997 General Election was the lowest for more than sixty years, and John Major fell on his sword immediately the result was announced.*

For the Tribune *of 4 April 1997 Martin Rowson produced an obvious - not to say revolting - image of the sleaze in which John Major had become stuck. Neil Hamilton was already causing problems for Major when the* Sun *reported that another Tory MP, Piers Merchant, had been having an affair with a teenage night-club hostess. John Major's response was to accuse Blair of dodging the real issues, and being too "chicken" to debate them with him. It does not do to examine too closely some of the elements floating around the Prime Minister, except to record that they take us back to the days of Gillray.*

On 6 April 1997 the Sunday Telegraph cartoon by "Trog" - Wally Fawkes - dealt with the launch of the Liberal Democrat manifesto two days earlier. Like the Labour and Conservative Manifestos, this promised increased spending on schools, but Paddy Ashdown was frank enough to admit that his ambitious programme would cost the average taxpayer 45p a week. The leap of shock comes from H.M. Bateman's famous series of cartoons "The Man Who...".

THE MAN WHO SAID TAX MIGHT HAVE TO RISE   after H.M. BATEMAN

democratisation of the Labour Party through "one member, one vote", but died suddenly of a heart attack in May 1994. Two months later the contest for a new leader was won not by another Scot, Gordon Brown, but by Tony Blair, who was thought by many in a party desperate for victory to be a more attractive personality, more presentable on television, and more likely to appeal to the voters. He spoke of inclusiveness while himself delivering strong leadership and gaining internal support for a united line on major issues.

The most important determining factor in the Labour campaign was that it had been defeated in the four previous General Elections - and that while the first three of those defeats had largely been expected, that of 1992 was a complete surprise. Blair formulated and constantly hammered home the idea of "New Labour", a reinvigorated party which could claim an explicit break with many of the idols, concepts and practices of "Old Labour". The dismantling of Old Labour deprived many cartoonists of their favourite targets - especially "Clause Four", which had been portrayed in many previous elections as Labour's threat to nationalise everything in sight, but would be absent from cartoons of the 1997 Election.

While Labour could and did revise itself because of four previous election defeats, the Conservative Party faced the problem of four successive wins. At first sight this might not seem a problem, but when combined with stories of sleaze and Cabinet conflict it reinforced the argument that it was "Time for a change".

Election Issues and the 1997 Campaign

John Major held on almost as long as was legally possible before calling the General Election, and even then he provided for a long campaign, running from 17 March to 1 May 1997. As with Callaghan in 1979, Major seems to have hoped that a long campaign would allow him to discredit

his opponents' policies, or at least would expose weaknesses and divisions within the recently-reconstructed Labour Party. However, the longest post-war Election campaign did not in fact produce bombshells or reveal issues of great impact on the electorate, and the opinion polls consistently showed Labour ahead by a long distance.

Sleaze continued to dog the Tory campaign. Neil Hamilton had resigned as a Minister over accusations that he had taken cash in brown envelopes from Mohammed Fayed in return for asking parliamentary questions, but he refused to give up his candidacy at Tatton. Here he was opposed by the "Anti-Corruption" candidate Martin Bell, in his famous white suit, whose confrontations with Hamilton and his formidable wife Christine kept sleaze in the forefront of the news. The Labour Party manifesto prudently included a promise to "clean up politics".

There were further problems for the Conservatives when newspapers that had staunchly supported them in the 1992 General Election came out for the Labour Party – or rather for Tony Blair. On the second day of the campaign the *Sun*, which famously claimed to have won the 1992 Election for Major, declared its support for Blair with a lengthy editorial declaring "The clapped-out Tories don't deserve to win...They have been tarnished with sleaze, riddled with scandal, beset by foolishness and weakened by division". Yet the only change in the quality of debate was to lower it even further below the level of previous elections. More than ever the media did not debate fundamental issues of difference between the parties, but focused on sound bites and abuse.

John Major and his Chancellor, Kenneth Clarke, attempted to control discussion of Britain's involvement in Europe, but failed as both backbenchers and then ministers broke ranks to insist that Britain should

In the Observer *of 6 April 1997 Chris Riddell dealt with the triumph of style over substance. John Major is back on the soapbox he used in 1992, but Tony Blair overshadows him with an ornate pulpit from which to deliver his message. This carries references t the fact that Blair was known to be a regular Churchgoer, and also to an element of preachiness in his style. A long history of Christian socialism was still reflected in New Labour - or at least the Christian bit was.*

Steve Bell's cartoon in the Guardian *of 9 April 1997 shows Neil Hamilton happily eating his way through a trough of money - apparently oblivious to the fact that it hangs on the edge of a cliff. On the previous day Hamilton had won his battle to stand in the General Election, but much of his local Conservative Party was against him, and only his formidable wife Christine seemed willing to stand beside him.*

Garland's Daily Telegraph *cartoon of 15 April 1997 links a threat to world fish stocks with the possible impact of the Election on the Conservative Party. Facing extinction are Portillo, Clarke, and Heseltine at the top, with Virginia Bottomley, Gillian Shepherd, and Howard below, following John Major, and Redwood, Rifkind, and Lamont cruising at the bottom behind Mawhinney. At this stage William Hague was not sufficiently notable to be included.*

never join the Euro. Major continued to attack Labour's proposals for constitutional reform, and in particular opposed devolution, regarding this stance as one of his successes in the 1992 Election. In contrast Tony Blair could portray devolution as giving the Scots and Welsh what most of them wanted. Labour also gave assurance of its economic probity - so often an issue in previous General Elections - by saying it would not increase income tax and would stick to Tory spending plans for two years. Blair also concentrated on social issues such as crime, pensions, and "education, education, education".

FISH STOCKS IN DANGER OF BEING WIPED OUT

Tony Blair writes of the 1997 General Election campaign: "General Elections - and certainly when you are personally involved - are usually exciting but always exhausting. And these two adjectives best describe my memories of the 1997 General Election campaign.

Exciting because the reaction we got as we criss-crossed the country, meeting and speaking to tens of thousands of people, was genuinely heart-warming. I've been in politics too long to believe the response on the ground automatically translates into votes in the ballot box, but there was no doubting the desire for change and a new beginning in the country.

Exhausting because it was a long campaign almost without a break – and certainly without a real rest. And exhausting also because so much depended on the outcome and so many people across the country were depending on our success.

I never thought the Election was in the bag. When I said every day of the campaign that I was not complacent about the outcome, I wasn't repeating a line. I truly believed it.

You can have the most carefully crafted strategy possible. Your party can be in good heart and ready for the battle ahead. The polls might show there is no way you can lose. All this was true for us in 1997. But that doesn't mean you ever take the voters for granted.

Complacency, fortunately, wasn't a danger with our party. Victory had eluded us for so long and we were so convinced that the country needed a new direction that there was never a danger that the party would relax.

But there always was a real fear that the polls might be wrong or that the public might take our victory for granted and stay at home rather than go to the polling booth. So we fought right to the end for every single seat – and every single vote – because we genuinely believed we might need it."

Graham High's cartoon in The Scotsman *of 18 April 1997 shows the Prime Minister tricking his Chancellor, Kenneth Clarke, with a false hand, while giving a real handshake to the Tory Eurosceptics. John Major had offered Tory MPs a free vote on European monetary union, at which two of his most senior colleagues - Kenneth Clarke and Michael Heseltine - complained that they had not been consulted beforehand.*

Peter Schrank's Independent cartoon of 28 April 1997 is a forecast of the inevitable Labour victory, where a tired John Major finds himself on the doorstep of No.10 blinking into the rising sun of Tony Blair's trademark smile. In retrospect the cartoon seems also to carry a reference to the day after the Election, when press photographers caught Cherie Blair on her own doorstep in her night-dress.

Personality of the 1997 General Election

Tony Blair

Tony Blair was the son of a successful barrister, who in the 1963 General Election suffered a stroke during a campaign to become a Conservative MP. Blair himself read law at Oxford, and qualified as a barrister before being elected as a Labour MP in the 1983 General Election.

The photographs of Tony Blair as a longhaired member of a pop band whilst at Oxford seemed more incredible than most student photographs of Prime Ministers. Yet musical ambitions were not the only ones that Blair shared with US President Bill Clinton, whose electoral success he studied. Both explicitly sought the centre ground, rather than relying on traditional ideology and bases within their political parties. Blair's movement to a more moderate centre ground, from traditional left wing views and support of CND during his early political life, was not unusual in the Labour Party. What was unusual, and what he and his supporters would claim underpinned the Labour victory of 1997, was that the move became an explicit statement of the new reality of Labour, rather than a pragmatic shift of opinion within the Labour Party or a Labour government.

Blair and Gordon Brown shared common views of how to move the Labour Party into electability, and when in 1994 the sudden death of John Smith demanded a new Labour leader, Brown was the more senior of the two. However, Brown accepted - no doubt with frustration - that Blair would be a more attractive leader for the wider electorate. Blair beat the more traditional Labour candidate John Prescott, and Margaret Beckett, to become party leader, and by 1997 he had established a clear image for himself. He was young, personable, and delivered the obligatory politician's attempts at sincerity extremely well. Like Kinnock he was prepared to take on those elements of the Labour Party he needed to beat in order to create an electable alternative to the Conservatives.

The removal of Clause Four in its old form from the Labour Party's Constitution was only symbolic, since Labour had long since abandoned it as a practical guide – but the symbol was seen to be very important. Blair was initially portrayed as Bambi by the

143

DOZENS OF HOSTAGES HELD FOR MONTHS IN FIGHT-TO-THE-DEATH...

Peter Brookes' Times *cartoon "Dozens of Hostages…," from 24 April 1997, carries a reference to the 126-day siege of the Japanese Ambassador's residence in Peru, which ended when troops rescued all but one of the hostages and killed their captors. Here Tony Blair and Peter Mandelson stand guard over their own long-term hostages - outspoken left-wingers held in silence during the Election campaign. It was felt that New Labour could not afford expressions of dissent, or even a mild diversity of views, and the hostages are John Prescott - an authoritative although occasionally incoherent representative of Old Labour, Dennis Skinner, Claire Short, Bill Morris - TGWU General Secretary representing the silence of the trade unions, Tony Benn, and Ken Livingstone.*

Steve Bell's cartoon of 2 May 1997 allowed Guardian *readers to say farewell to John Major through a particularly powerful image. The viking funeral of Major's underpants carries echoes of J.M.W. Turner's 1834 painting "The Burning of the Houses of Parliament".*

TORY 'A'

A TORY HAS JUST BEEN RETURNED TO Nº 10

BUT CAN YOU TELL THE DIFFERENCE AND PUT THE RIGHT P.M. IN OFFICE ?

TORY 'B'

CUT OUT THE 2 TORY HEADS PLACE PIN THRU. HOLE 'X' (WHERE IT WILL DO LEAST DAMAGE)

WHILE BLINDFOLDED ATTEMPT TO AFFIX APPROPRIATE HEAD IN APPROPRIATE POSITION

THE WINNER ? DON'T BE SILLY WE ALL LOSE !

Dave Brown's "Pin the Head on the Tory", from the Independent *of 2 May 1997 was a cartoon that proved uncomfortably prophetic for some Labour voters - and they were not the only ones to feel uneasy about the image. In Brown's original drawing the right-hand box ended with the words "The winner? Don't be silly we all lose!", but the paper's editor removed the final three words before publication, and then dropped the entire cartoon from the second edition for giving the wrong impression of Labour's victory.*

political cartoonists, but well before the General Election of 1997 he had shown that this image of innocence was ludicrously inappropriate.

The Results of the 1997 General Election

The 1997 General Election saw a dramatic collapse in the Tory vote, and the impact was increased by significant tactical voting for Labour and the Liberal Democrats. The Labour Party won a landslide in seats if not in votes, and secured a commanding majority. Equally significantly, 101 of the 418 Labour members were women, although this major shift in gender was slow to make any significant cultural change in the House of Commons. Turnout was 71.2% - the lowest in any post-war Election - and the detailed results were:

Labour	418	43.2%
Conservative	165	30.7%
Liberal Democrats	46	16.8%
Welsh and Scottish Nationalists	10	2.5%
Others	20	6.8%

The Cartoonist of the 1997 General Election

Steve Bell has been chosen as the cartoonist of the 1997 General Election, largely for his success in skewering John Major. Bell's main outlet for his cartoons is the *Guardian*, which he joined as political cartoonist in 1990, and in the same year he was looking for an image of Major, when he hit upon the idea of drawing him as "a crap Superman" - someone who thought he was a super hero, but instead of a Superman kit just wore underpants over his trousers. A story later emerged that Major had committed the sartorial solecism of tucking his shirt into his underpants, and although Bell's cartoons were not based on this rumour they certainly benefited from it.

Unlike Vicky, whose attempt to satirise Harold Macmillan as "Supermac" proved counterproductive, Bell's portrayal of John Major in his underpants was both cruel and effective. It was in fact so successful that it may be a relief to Bell in more ways than one that John Major has disappeared from the scene, as he may not wish to be forever associated with Major's underpants, brilliant though the metaphor was. However, Bell's work during the 1997 general Election had a wider range, and amongst the many cartoons attacking political sleaze, his portrayal of Neil Hamilton in the *Guardian* on 9 April 1997 was vicious and direct.

Steve Bell is held in high regard by many of his fellow cartoonists, and although his strong social and political views might offend even some *Guardian* readers, the emphatic and occasionally grotesque style in which they are expressed gives them an added fascination and a wider impact. In discussion with the author, Bell explained that his experience with his *Guardian* editors - Peter Preston and Alan Rusbridger - has been that they give him a free hand with his cartoons and provide support when necessary. He rarely goes to editorial conferences, partly because he works from home, but also because he does not need to have ideas offered to him.

Copyright in the Cartoons

The Centre for the Study of Cartoons and Caricature is grateful to all the copyright holders who generously gave permission for cartoons to appear in this book, and whose names appear below. Every effort has been made to trace the remaining copyright holders, but unfortunately without success.

"Abu" (Abu Abraham) by kind permission of the cartoonist, page 37 (top).

Steve Bell by kind permission of the cartoonist, pages 131 (top), 141 (top), and 144 (bottom).

Peter Brookes by kind permission of the cartoonist and © News International, pages 109 and 144 (top).

Dave Brown by kind permission of the cartoonist, pages 137 and 145.

Michael Cummings by kind permission of © Express Newspapers, pages 13, 17, 21 (top), 23, 32 (top), 38, 40, 43, 49 (top), 51, 54, 64 (bottom), 65 (top), 71 (top), 78 (bottom), 82 (bottom), 88 (bottom), 90 (top), 94, 95, 97, 100 (bottom), 101 (top), 107 (bottom), 110 (top), 120 (top and bottom), 121, 125, and 127.

"Eccles" (Frank Brown) by kind permission of Sid Brown, pages 60 (top), 74 (top), 79, and 92.

"Emmwood" (John Musgrave-Wood) by kind permission of © Solo Syndication/Associated Newspapers, pages 42 (bottom), 73, 82 (top), and 88 (top).

Stanley Franklin by kind permission of *The Sun*, pages 47, 99 (top), 102 (top), 108 (bottom), 114 (top), and 133.

George Gale, pages 60 (bottom) and 107 (top).

Nick Garland by kind permission of *The Daily Telegraph*, pages 62, 64 (top), 75 (bottom), 77, 78 (top), 124 (bottom), 129 (top), 138 (top), and 141 (bottom).

Dave Gaskill by kind permission of the cartoonist, page 132.

David Ghilchik, page 15.

Les Gibbard by kind permission of the cartoonist, pages 84, 89, 110 (bottom), 113, 123, and 126.

Charles Griffin by kind permission of the cartoonist, page 131 (bottom).

Graham High, page 142.

Leslie Illingworth by kind permission of © Solo Syndication/Associated Newspapers, pages 6, 11,28, 30 and 44: and by kind permission of © Punch Ltd, pages 4 (bottom), 12, 19, 24 (top), 27, 28, 31 (top), 48-9 (bottom), 57, 61, and 90 (bottom).

"Jak" (Raymond Jackson) by kind permission of © Solo Syndication/Associated Newspapers, pages 66 (top), 80 (top and bottom), 87 (top), 101 (bottom), and 112.

John Jensen by kind permission of the cartoonist, page iv and by kind permission of *The Daily Telegraph*, pages 52 (bottom), 59, 69 (top), 70, and 91 (top).

"Jon" (William John Philpin Jones) by kind permission of Sylvia Philpin Jones, pages 22 (bottom), and 25.

"Kal" (Kevin Kallaugher) by kind permission of the cartoonist, pages vii and 118 (bottom).

David Low by kind permission of © Solo Syndication/Associated Newspapers, pages 4 (top), 7, 9, 14 (top and bottom), 18, 20 (bottom), 32 (bottom), 42 (top), and 45.

"Mac" (Stan McMurtry) by kind permission of © Solo Syndication/Associated Newspapers, pages 114 (bottom) and 118 (top).

Kenneth Mahood by kind permission of © Punch Ltd, page 69 (bottom).

Norman Mansbridge by kind permission of © Punch Ltd, page 66 (bottom).

Sidney Moon, page 29 (bottom).

Bill Papas by kind permission of Tessa Papas , pages 48 (top), 56, 63 (top) and 68 (top) and © Punch Ltd page 67 (bottom).

Chris Riddell by kind permission of the cartoonist, pages 130, 134 (bottom), and 140.

Paul Rigby, pages 74 (bottom), 81 (top), 85 (bottom), and 91 (bottom).

Rodger, page 16 (top).

Stephen Roth, page 3 (top).

Martin Rowson by kind permission of the cartoonist, pages 119, 128, and 138 (bottom).

Willie Rushton by kind permission of Toby Rushton, pages 129 (bottom), and 134 (top).

Peter Schrank by kind permission of the cartoonist, page 143.

Ernest Shepard by kind permission of © Punch Ltd, page 2.

Ralph Steadman by kind permission of the cartoonist, cover and pages 72, 98, 116, and 122.

Sidney "George" Strube by kind permission of © Express Newspapers, pages 5 (top), 8, and 35.

"Trog" (Wally Fawkes) by kind permission of the cartoonist, pages 52 (top), 63 (bottom), 67 (top), 68 (bottom), 85 (top), 93, 105 (top), 108 (top), 117, 124 (top), 136, and 139.

"Vicky" (Victor Weisz) by kind permission of © Solo Syndication/Associated Newspapers, pages 1, 3 (bottom), 5 (bottom), 16 (bottom), 20 (top), 22 (top), 24 (bottom), 29 (top), 31 (bottom), 33, 34, 37 (bottom), 41 (top), 50 (top and bottom), 53, and 55.

Keith Waite by kind permission of the cartoonist, pages 99 (bottom), 100 (top), and 102 (bottom).

Philip Zec by kind permission of © Mirror Group Newspapers, page 39.

"Zoke" (Michael Attwell), page 115.